Inviting Children's Responses to Literature

Inviting Children's Responses to Literature

Guides to 57 Notable Books

Edited by

Amy A. McClure
Ohio Wesleyan University

Janice V. Kristo
University of Maine

National Council of Teachers of English
1111 West Kenyon Road, Urbana, Illinois 61801-1096

Editors: Michael E. Himick and Marlo Welshons

Cover Designer: Victoria Martin Pohlmann

Interior Book Designer: Doug Burnett

NCTE Stock Number 23791-3050

Library of Congress Cataloging-in-Publication Data

Inviting children's responses to literature : guides to 57 notable
  books / edited by Amy A. McClure, Janice V. Kristo.
    p. cm.
   "NCTE stock number 23791-3050"—T.p. verso.
   Includes bibliographical references.
   ISBN 0-8141-2379-1 : $12.95/$9.95
    1. Literature—Study and teaching (Elementary)—United States.
  2. Children—United States—Books and reading. 3. Language arts
(Elementary)—United States. I. McClure, Amy A. II. Kristo,
Janice V.
  LA1575.5.U6I58   1994
  372.64—dc20   93-46088
                                           CIP

Contents

Acknowledgments   xi

Introduction   xiii

1. *Amazing Grace*
   Rachael Hungerford   1

2. *Animalia*
   Cheryl Grossman   3

3. *Anno's U.S.A.*
   Inga Kromann-Kelly   5

4. *Balloons and Other Poems*
   Amy McClure and Linda Leonard Lamme   7

5. *The Best Town in the World*
   Inga Kromann-Kelly   9

6. *The Book of Pigericks*
   Inga Kromann-Kelly   12

7. *Brave Irene*
   Janice Kristo and Melissa Keenan   14

8. *The Cat's Purr*
   Joan I. Glazer   16

9. *The Celery Stalks at Midnight*
   Inga Kromann-Kelly   18

10. *Chicka Chicka Boom Boom*
    Carol Avery   21

11. *Dear Mr. Henshaw*
    Inga Kromann-Kelly   23

12. *The Dove's Letter*
    Cheryl Grossman   26

13. *The Eleventh Hour: A Curious Mystery*
    Susan Lehr   28

14. *Feathers for Lunch*
    Carol Avery   30

15. *Flossie and the Fox*
    Janice Kristo and Melissa Keenan   32

16. *Foolish Rabbit's Big Mistake*
    Joan I. Glazer   34

17. *Frank and Ernest*
    Cheryl Grossman   36

18. *Galimoto*
    Linda Leonard Lamme   38

19. *The Ghost-Eye Tree*
    Joan I. Glazer   40

20. *The Green Lion of Zion Street*
    Darwin L. Henderson   42

21. *Halloween ABC*
    Cheryl Grossman   44

22. *Heartland*
    Linda Leonard Lamme   46

23. *Heckedy Peg*
    Cheryl Grossman   48

24. *The High Rise Glorious Skittle Skat Roarious
    Sky Pie Angel Food Cake*
    Carol Avery   50

25. *If You Were a Writer*
    Carolyn J. Bauer   52

26. *I'm in Charge of Celebrations*
    Marilou R. Sorensen   54

27. *In the Year of the Boar and Jackie Robinson*
    Richard Van Dongen and Jill P. May   56

28. *The Island*
    Jon C. Stott   58

29. *The Jolly Postman; or, Other People's Letters*
    Cheryl Grossman   60

30. *Joyful Noise: Poems for Two Voices*
    Amy McClure   63

31. *Knots on a Counting Rope*
    Cheryl Grossman   65

32. *Little Tricker the Squirrel Meets Big
    Double the Bear*
    Carol Avery   68

33. *Lyddie*
    Rachael Hungerford   70

34. *The Magical Adventures of Pretty Pearl*
    Inga Kromann-Kelly   72

35. *The Mysteries of Harris Burdick*
    Marilou R. Sorensen   74

36. *Nettie's Trip South*
    Cheryl Grossman   76

37. *The News about Dinosaurs*
    Sylvia M. Vardell   78

38. *One-Eyed Cat*
    Jill P. May and Inga Kromann-Kelly   81

39. *The People Could Fly: American Black Folktales*
    Joan I. Glazer and Richard Van Dongen   83

40. *Red Leaf, Yellow Leaf*
    Rachael Hungerford   85

41. *The Remembering Box*
    Joan I. Glazer   87

42. *Return to Bitter Creek*
    Joan I. Glazer   89

43. *Sarah, Plain and Tall*
    Joan I. Glazer   91

44. *The Secret Language of Snow*
    Marilou R. Sorensen   93

45. *Small Poems Again*
    Amy McClure   95

46. *The Spring of Butterflies and Other Folktales
    of China's Minority Peoples*
    Anthony L. Manna   97

47. *The Talking Eggs: A Folktale from the
    American South*
    Susan Lehr   100

48. *Tar Beach*
    Rachael Hungerford   102

49. *Thunder Cake*
    Carol Avery   104

50. *The True Confessions of Charlotte Doyle*
    Carol Avery and Carl Tomlinson   106

51. *Tuesday*
    Rachael Hungerford   110

52. *Waiting to Waltz: A Childhood*
    Anthony L. Manna and Jill P. May   112

53. *The Wall*
    Carol Avery   114

54. *We're Going on a Bear Hunt*
    Darwin L. Henderson   116

55. *Whiskers and Rhymes*
    Joan I. Glazer   118

56. *The Winter Room*
    Carol Avery   120

57. *Woodsong*
    Carol Avery   122

Bibliography of Notable Books   125

Editors   141

Contributors   142

Acknowledgments

The editors gratefully acknowledge the assistance and hard work of Amy Cates, Sara Sheppard, Doreen Thibodeau, Melissa Keenan, and Rebecca Long of the University of Maine and Patricia Chilcoat and Laurie George of Ohio Wesleyan University.

The editors also extend their appreciation to Michael Spooner and Michelle Sanden Johlas of the National Council of Teachers of English.

Introduction

Amy A. McClure and Janice V. Kristo

When children come to school, they bring all sorts of "baggage" with them along with their coats and lunchboxes. Among other things, they have strong needs to feel good about themselves and to make sense of the world. Reading good literature, and then responding to it through talk, writing, and drama, helps them to begin to figure out how the world works and what their place is in it. These response guides, created by members of the Notable Children's Trade Books in the Language Arts Committee, were developed to provide teachers with ideas to guide this process.

The Notable Children's Trade Books in the Language Arts Committee is affiliated with the Children's Literature Assembly of the National Council of Teachers of English. The goal of this committee is to annually select the most outstanding trade books for enhancing language development among elementary and middle school children. Books considered for the Notables list must meet several of the following criteria:

1. They must deal explicitly with language, perhaps using devices such as plays-on-words or offering insight into word origins or the history of language.

2. They must demonstrate uniqueness in their use of language.

3. They must evoke participatory response from elementary children, have an appealing format, and meet the generally accepted criteria of quality for the genres in which they were written.

Committee members also strive to include a diverse mix of genres, including poetry, historical fiction, picture books, realistic fiction, fantasy, folktales, biographies, and nonfiction.

From each year's list we have selected the titles that committee members thought were the most enduring—that is, those most appealing to children as well as useful to teachers. The response guides were then created to provide teachers with ideas for helping children respond more thoughtfully to the books. We hope that you will find them to be rich resources for furthering children's growth in using language imaginatively.

Philosophy

We believe that a good guide should deepen a reader's response to a book by providing opportunities for using language to express and develop that response. Our activities are thus designed to help children clarify their understanding by returning to the book to find evidence to support their ideas. We also hope that children will extend their understanding as they compare a book to others they have read or to their own experiences, and we have provided ideas for doing this through all the language arts: conversation, writing, reading, and listening.

Louise Rosenblatt's milestone work, *Literature as Exploration* (1938), greatly influenced our thinking in the formulation of the response guides. This landmark book helped to establish a different way of thinking about the role of reader, text, and teacher. Rosenblatt envisioned a much more active role for the reader, one which capitalizes on the power of the reader to bring meaning to a text. She defined reading as a transactional process, one in which the reader brings many experiences to a book and, thus, a personal interpretation to the reading. This is not to say that all meaning resides in the reader, but that the reader needs to return to the text to test out hypotheses and interpretations. In other words, to what extent does the reader's response make sense in light of the text? Thus, a dynamic transaction between text and reader occurs. Rosenblatt also conceived of the reader's stance as being either aesthetic—reading for personal response—or efferent—reading for analytic or critical purposes. The suggestions found in our guides invite response from both of these stances.

Keeping Rosenblatt's ideas in mind, we believe that it is crucial to begin with the reader's "agenda." We suggest that a good starting point is to invite conversation about the initial reactions readers have to a book. For instance, in the foreword to *Children Talking about Books* (Borders and Naylor 1993), Jacque Touchton states, "I believe the most rewarding experience in teaching reading is hearing the delight in children's voices as they describe a story and its connection to their inner worlds." Borders and Naylor suggest the use of three discussion prompts that allow readers to react in this way: What did you notice about the story? How did the story make you feel? What does the story remind you of in your own life?

Similarly, Peterson and Eeds, in *Grand Conversations: Literature Groups in Action* (1990), discuss the value of personal response by stating, "We want children not only to learn how to read, but also to become readers. We consider children's enjoyment and interpretation of literature to be our foremost concern." They further suggest that "genuine meaning, meaning over which readers have ownership, arises only if those readers are able to structure it themselves, through their own interpretations, in the light of their experiences and their intent." Thus, Peterson and Eeds also advocate dialogue as the way into text interpretation. Teachers can initiate "grand conversations" with students by first inviting them to talk about their personal responses. Then they can use these responses as the basis for further dialogue, dialogue that seeks to uncover layers of meaning in plot, character, setting, point of view, time, and mood. This suggests beginning with the kinds of questions that tap what children think and feel about a book, what they wondered about, and what they liked. The reader's responses to these types of questions will then lead to further discussion about literary characteristics. As Peterson and Eeds note, "The tone of the sharing shifts at this point, because to respond to this question the children need to analyze, interpret, and seek out evidence for their positions." This moves the reader from a personal, or aesthetic, response to a more analytic, or efferent, one.

This perspective suggests that teachers must move away from the more typical kinds of comprehension questions that one often finds in such materials as basal readers and exhaustive published guides to trade books. These questions are predetermined by a publisher and do not emerge from authentic book conversation. In fact, some researchers are exploring whether certain types of questioning actually impede comprehension. We are concerned about the "basalization" of trade books. A fifty-page guide to Arnold Lobel's *Frog and Toad* series or Eric Carle's *The Very Hungry Caterpillar* (1969), complete with worksheets, page-by-page analysis, questions that quiz children on every conceivable aspect of the story, and cutesy art activities, "basalizes" literature and does not cultivate enjoyment of books. These kinds of "chores" to do with a book send children the wrong message about the value of literature and stifle personal response to books.

Allington and Weber (1993) similarly question the instructional cycle that arises when teachers ask questions drawn mainly from manuals, expect students to respond, and then evaluate these responses. For them, such routines lead to a highly structured, routinized cycle that taps only a superficial interpretation of what was read. They further state that such "routines do not allow for questions that reveal ignorance, request clarification, puzzle over meaning, express curiosity, draw comparisons, or raise hypotheses on the part of either students or teachers." As an alternative, they too suggest posing authentic puzzlements and curiosities about the reading. Thus, a conversation about Patricia MacLachlan's *Sarah, Plain and Tall* (1985) might go like this: "Sarah made me think of the time I moved to the Midwest from New England. I missed the ocean and landscape, much as Sarah did. Have any of you had a similar kind of experience?" This kind of talk is much closer to the authentic conversations that adults have about books with one another. Those discussions are, of course, not stilted or interrogative but personal in nature: "So, what do you think of the story?" "I loved the part when . . ." "Have you read anything else by this author?"

Thus, our activities are not designed to follow any hierarchy or taxonomy. We've omitted vocabulary lists, fill-in-the-blank exercises, and comprehension questions because we wanted the emphasis to be on open-ended activities that encourage rich conversations about books. Our intent is to help stimulate children's talking and thinking, not tap their ability to find a right answer or color in the lines.

In *Booktalk* (1985), Aidan Chambers offers a host of interesting and challenging questions that promise to stimulate some rich conversations within a "Tell Me Framework": Tell me, when you first saw the book, even before you read it, what kind of book did you think it was going to be? Tell me about anything that particularly caught your attention. What will you tell your friends about it? Tell me about the parts you liked most. Tell me about the parts you didn't like. Was there anything that puzzled you? Chambers also eschews the use of the word *why* as a follow-up to a reader's response to a question, as he says that this word tends to box in the reader, putting the student in a defensive posture. Instead, he suggests using the phrase "Tell me more about how you're thinking." Try this sometime; it takes a lot of practice. As teachers, we are so used to following up a student response with the ubiquitous *why*.

What then is the role of the teacher in a more response-centered classroom? The teacher becomes a more active participant in discussions, an enthusiastic reader who voices responses just as the students do. Thus, the teacher is a collaborator in the meaning-making process. As Peterson and Eeds (1990) so aptly state:

> Teachers work alongside their students, negotiate meaning with them, and take into account their perspectives—what they know and don't know. Information is supplied to fill specific needs and meaning simplified to sustain inquiry. Certainly this is the most difficult and challenging kind of teaching. Teachers must be listeners who avoid domination and act collaboratively. They must trust that, by collaborating, students will not only learn about literature, but also practice a process of acting and reflecting— making inquiries and critiquing—that will help them learn how to learn.

Borders and Naylor (1993) also advocate this role for teachers in literature discussion groups. They state, "The real work of the adult in the group is to LISTEN, LISTEN, LISTEN. The children are working at creating meaning for themselves. By listening carefully, our own reflections can be carefully phrased to stimulate higher levels of thinking or at least more informed reflections."

With all this in mind, what is the place of the response guides you will find in this book? We envision these guides neither as starting points nor as ending places. What we do advocate as a starting place is lots of rich conversation with children about books from the guides. Returning to the notion of the reader's "agenda," we invite you to formulate the kinds of questions, such as those discussed above, that invite authentic booktalk among all readers, including the teacher. We see wisdom in Border's (1993) decision "to give up *directing* children how to communicate, make choices, 'say no,' and act assertively."

Take time to discover how your students think and feel about a book. Trust the power of a good book to move readers, to spark their imagination, and to steer them on a course of discovery and adventure. As Borders and Naylor (1993) note, "The children take the discussions in directions that win our unending admiration. We often find that the fewer prompts we use, the better the discussion. The more we make comments instead of questions, the more comments the children make. The less we talk, the more the children will talk."

We hope that you will use the ideas in these response guides as ways to build *from* your group's agenda, to deepen conversations, and to invite children to consider new response opportunities. We are continually amazed at the stimulating conversations and extraordinary insights that evolve when children are given the time and opportunity to ponder real questions about their reading. We've also discovered that when we allow children to talk and write in connection with books, they often create their own agendas for where to go next.

The response suggestions offered in the guides that follow have been carefully crafted. They capitalize on the rich language qualities of each book and work on the principle of integration of the language arts. Our intent is to invite readers to look at books through the eyes of a writer. If readers enjoyed a book, what did the author do in terms of the effective use of language and the crafting of plot, characters, setting, and so forth that so successfully pulled them in to the world of the book?

Format   Each guide is composed of four sections: suggested grade levels, a plot summary, teaching suggestions, and a list of related books.

Suggested Grade Levels

We think it's helpful to have an idea of the typical level at which a book might be used. Nonetheless, the grade levels we've indicated for each book are merely guidelines. We feel strongly that a book can appeal to a wide range of ages if it meets a particular child's emotional needs or current interests.

Plot Summary

We've identified significant aspects of the story and categorized each book according to genre or theme. We've also tried to provide a sense of literary quality, focusing particularly on the book's language and its capacity to evoke language from children.

Teaching Suggestions

These are the heart of our guides. We've provided ideas mainly to help children use language in different ways to think about books. Thus, we have suggested a variety of teaching strategies: dramatization, shared storytelling, comparison charting, storymapping, letter and journal writing, and the like. We've also tried to use all the different modes of the language arts so that readers can develop their reading, speaking, writing, and listening skills using authentic texts. Our most important goal, however, was to develop activities that genuinely stimulated critical thinking, leading readers to new insights that prompt them to say, "I never thought of it that way before" or "That reminds me of . . ." or "I want to learn more about . . ." We also continually asked ourselves whether a child would learn more from doing an activity. Would it make the book more meaningful or more memorable? Would it motivate children to return to the book for rereadings or clarification of ideas? Would it be rewarding, fun, challenging, and enriching?

Related Books

This section was designed to suggest resources that could extend an idea or theme related to a particular book. It is often difficult to stay current when so many new titles are published each year. It is also a challenge to identify those books that relate to one another or to a specific theme. Therefore, we have tried to remedy this situation by suggesting titles that seem to work well for extension activities and that will expand your students' reading horizons. Our suggestions are not meant to be exhaustive, but rather are starting points from which to stimulate your thinking.

We want your community of readers to discover how words can express just the right feeling, make characters come alive, or help them discover what makes them human as they chart their reading travels, both to the world they know and to places they have yet to discover. One final word: As a teacher, please chart a reading voyage for yourself as well. You may well make some important discoveries about yourself as a reader too!

References

Professional Resources

Allington, Richard L., and Rose-Marie Weber. 1993. "Questioning Questions in Teaching and Learning from Texts." In *Learning from Textbooks: Theory and Practice*, edited by Bruce K. Britton, Arthur Woodward, and Marilyn Binkley, 47–68. Hillsdale, NJ: Lawrence Erlbaum Associates.

Borders, Sarah G., and Alice Phoebe Naylor. 1993. *Children Talking about Books*. Phoenix: Oryx Press.

Chambers, Aidan. 1985. *Booktalk: Occasional Writing on Literature and Children*. New York: Harper and Row.

Peterson, Ralph L., and Maryann Eeds. 1990. *Grand Conversations: Literature Groups in Action*. New York: Scholastic.

Rosenblatt, Louise M. 1983 [1938]. *Literature as Exploration*. 4th ed. New York: Modern Language Association.

Children's Literature

Carle, Eric. 1969. *The Very Hungry Caterpillar*. New York: Philomel Books.

Lobel, Arnold. 1970. *Frog and Toad Are Friends*. New York: Harper and Row.

————. 1972. *Frog and Toad Together*. New York: Harper and Row.

————. 1976. *Frog and Toad All Year*. New York: Harper and Row.

————. 1979. *Days with Frog and Toad*. New York: Harper and Row.

MacLachlan, Patricia. 1985. *Sarah, Plain and Tall*. New York: Harper and Row.

Amazing Grace

Mary Hoffman. *Amazing Grace.* Illustrated by Caroline Binch.
New York: Dial Books, 1991. ISBN 0-8037-1040-2.

Suggested Grade Levels: 1–3

Plot Summary

Grace *is* amazing. Joyously involved in stories of every kind, Grace loves stories from books, stories from movies, stories her grandmother tells. Whether it's Joan of Arc, Mowgli, Hiawatha, or Anansi the Spider, she gives herself the most exciting part and acts it out with intense delight and energy. She is sure that she can be anything she wants to be. But when Grace announces her intention of being Peter Pan in the class play, her classmates discourage her because she is a "girl" and because she is "black." Ma and Nana support Grace's desire and independence with love and strong examples. The result is that Grace *can* be anything she wants to be, including Peter Pan.

This book is amazing as well, especially in the remarkable and positive possibilities it offers to readers. Grace, Ma, and Nana are all strong female characters: supportive, loving, and actively creating a life and family of their own. Issues of gender and race are addressed frankly. The other stories and characters Grace enjoys are referred to with just enough brevity to tease readers into wanting to find out more about them (e.g., "Grace went into battle as Joan of Arc and wove a wicked web as Anansi the Spider"). The language is clear, concise, and well chosen to move the story forward quickly.

Teaching Suggestions

1. Children could find and read the stories referred to in the book. Then they might chart characteristics of the various stories and characters in order to discover why Grace finds them so appealing.

2. This book offers many opportunities for discussion of race and gender issues.

3. Children could create a list of characteristics that describe first Grace and then themselves as amazing. From this list they

could create a descriptive paragraph, poem, song, or collage about Grace or themselves.

4. Acronyms are an easy beginning poetry form that children could write around Grace's name. Each word chosen to describe Grace might indicate how she is amazing. The children could also create "amazing" acronyms for their own names and illustrate them with self-portraits.

5. Children could choose their favorite storybook character and dramatize that character as Grace does. They might also write a short script for their character. Such a "story drama" could be presented to other classes or for parents.

Related Books

Other books that focus on self-concept for young children:

Adoff, Arnold. *Hard To Be Six.*

Blume, Judy. *The Pain and the Great One.*

Carlson, Nancy. *I Like Me.*

Cleary, Beverly. *Ramona the Brave.*

Frasier, Debra. *On the Day You Were Born.*

Giff, Patricia Reilly. *Today Was a Terrible Day.*

Glen, Maggie. *Ruby.*

Grifalconi, Ann. *Darkness and the Butterfly.*

Heide, Florence Parry. *The Shrinking of Treehorn.*

Henkes, Kevin. *Chrysanthemum.*

Hughes, Shirley. *An Evening at Alfie's.*

Keats, Ezra Jack. *Whistle for Willie.*

Kellogg, Steven. *Much Bigger than Martin.*

Kraus, Robert. *Leo the Late Bloomer.*

Lionni, Leo. *Frederick.*

Mills, Lauren. *The Rag Coat.*

Ringgold, Faith. *Tar Beach.*

Sharmat, Marjorie. *I'm the Best!*

—by Rachael Hungerford

Animalia

Graeme Base. *Animalia.* New York: Harry N. Abrams, 1987. ISBN 0-8109-1868-4.

Suggested Grade Levels: 3–6

Plot Summary

If the thought of "ingenious iguanas improvising an intricate impromptu on impossible instruments" stimulates your imagination, then you will applaud this inventive and visually stunning alphabet book. From A to Z, the reader encounters fascinating animals in exotic settings and situations described in alliterative language. Each illustration contains detailed images of things that begin with the letter depicted on that page. For example, for the letter T, not only does the reader view "two tigers taking the 10:20 train to Timbuktu," but a closer look also shows a toad on a tricycle, a tortoise playing a tuba, toucans at a tavern, and much more as well. As an added incentive for careful viewing, Graeme Base as a young boy is "hidden" in each illustration, tempting the reader to find him. This is an alphabet book that will appeal to all ages, encouraging discussion about and reexamination of both the text and the illustrations.

Teaching Suggestions

1. This book will certainly inspire children to write and illustrate their own ABC book using alliteration and detailed, bizarre illustrations in the style of Graeme Base.

2. Because the illustrations and text have an "anything-may-happen" quality, they could act as stimuli for the writing of imaginative stories, stories that might then evolve into dramatic presentations.

3. The juxtaposition of fantastic images in each of Base's illustrations adds a surreal feeling to his artwork. Teachers could introduce the works of surrealistic artists such as Giorgio de Chirico, Max Ernst, and Salvador Dali to the class. Then students could be encouraged to conduct further research into the surrealist movement and to share their findings. Students might enjoy creating and then naming surrealistic collages inspired by their research and constructed from magazine images.

4. Base does not simplify his vocabulary for the reader. He often uses words that children may not be familiar with, words such as *diabolical, intricate, meticulous, queuing, vociferous,* and *vexatiously.* Children could be challenged to predict the meaning of these words from their context and then to check their accuracy using a dictionary. As an added challenge, encourage children to browse through the dictionary to find words they do not know but that appeal to them. Invite the children to use two or three of the words in a sentence. The sentences might then be written on strips, illustrated, and shared with other class members. Another possibility is to write the word in a way that somehow conveys its meaning. For example, *quivering* might be scrawled with a shaky hand, whereas *enormous* could scream out its size in gigantic letters.

Related Books

Other alphabet books with interesting formats:

Baskin, Hosie, Tobias Baskin, and Lisa Baskin. *Hosie's Alphabet.*

Bayer, Jane. *A, My Name Is Alice.*

Chouinard, Roger. *The Amazing Animal Alphabet Book.*

Dragonwagon, Crescent. *Alligator Arrived with Apples: A Potluck Alphabet Feast.*

Ehlert, Lois. *Eating the Alphabet: Fruits and Vegetables from A to Z.*

Geisert, Arthur. *Pigs from A to Z.*

Grover, Max. *The Accidental Zucchini: An Unexpected Alphabet.*

Kellogg, Steven. *Aster Aardvark's Alphabet Adventures.*

Lobel, Anita. *Alison's Zinnia.*

MacDonald, Suse. *Alphabatics.*

Purviance, Susan, and Marcia O'Shell. *Alphabet Annie Announces an All-American Album.*

Rankin, Laura. *The Handmade Alphabet.*

Van Allsburg, Chris. *The Z Was Zapped: A Play in Twenty-Six Acts.*

—by Cheryl Grossman

Anno's U.S.A.

Mitsumasa Anno. *Anno's U.S.A.* New York: Philomel Books, 1983. ISBN 0-399-20974-3.

Suggested Grade Levels: 2–8

Plot Summary

In this wordless book, Anno takes readers on a journey of discovery across the United States, exploring dimensions of history, geography, and culture by means of detailed watercolor and ink illustrations that juxtapose different times and settings. Moving from west to east and back in time, the book shows the cities, villages, and landscapes that serve as the backdrop for people at work and at play: taking goods to the market, a cattle roundup, a jazz session, a wedding, a harvest festival, a parade. The cast of characters includes such famous persons as Benjamin Franklin, Louisa May Alcott, and Laurel and Hardy as well as characters from literature, folklore, and film. Filled with puzzles and humor, this celebration of America reveals new discoveries with each reading.

Teaching Suggestions

1. Children could develop a web focusing on such elements as the settings, characters, time periods, and events featured in the book. Such an activity naturally leads to further research, where children might want to verify or elaborate on facts of interest. Pictures without a specified context, such as the raising of the flag at Iwo Jima, could send students scurrying to resources for details.

2. Using the above information, students could discuss what they feel are the most significant events portrayed in the book and then plot them on both a time line and a map of the United States.

3. Children could try to identify all the literary characters shown, from Paul Bunyan to Tom Sawyer to Maurice Sendak. Then they could check in the "Afterward" for any they missed. Children could speculate about why these particular characters were included and what other characters might have been included. Have children read the books in which these characters appear.

4. Art and architecture are important dimensions of culture. Children could be encouraged to find well-known American buildings, sculptures, and paintings in Anno's book. Then they could find pictures of these in books on art and architecture.

Related Books

The following books also detail changes in an area or country:

Anno, Mitsumasa. *Anno's Journey.*

Burton, Virginia Lee. *The Little House.*

Dragonwagon, Crescent. *Home Place.*

Goodall, John S. *Above and Below Stairs.*

Goodall, John S. *The Story of an English Village.*

McLerran, Alice. *Roxaboxen.*

Provensen, Alice, and Martin Provensen. *Shaker Lane.*

Shulevitz, Uri. *Toddlecreek Post Office.*

—by Inga Kromann-Kelly

Balloons and Other Poems

Deborah Chandra. *Balloons and Other Poems.* Illustrated by Leslie Bowman. New York: Farrar, Straus and Giroux, 1990. ISBN 0-374-30509-9.

Suggested Grade Levels: 3–8

Plot Summary

This book of poetry invites children to delight in the vivid, intriguing images of the world around them. The twenty-four poems that make up the collection are unusual in their use of language to create those images. For example, the title poem opens the collection with the following as its first verse: "Such swollen creatures, / Holding their breath / While they swim / Dreamily from / Room to room . . ." The final poem, "Night," begins "Silently / The night / Surrounds me, / Folds its soft / Dark around me . . ." Between are poems with titles such as "Fireworks," "Skeleton," "The Sea," "The Purr," "Mama's Song," and "Stray Dog." Skin is compared to "a canvas tent that's stretched from bone to bone," while autumn leaves are described as "grieving for summer with sighs and gasps." Each poem is exquisitely crafted and begs to be read again and again for both the musical quality of the words and the gentle invitation to ponder the ideas expressed.

Teaching Suggestions

1. Chandra's work is particularly noteworthy for its use of metaphorical language. Children could be asked to discuss this language and then to make a chart of all the unusual yet appropriate words and phrases Chandra uses to create her images.

2. Children could create their own poems about common, everyday objects. First they could be encouraged to generate a list of unusual words and phrases to describe their object. Then teachers could guide them in placing these words into a pleasing poetic arrangement.

3. Sometimes a teacher could invite children to close their eyes and visualize the images a poem evokes as it is read aloud.

Some children may wish to share these images later. They might even draw them as an option for responding.

4. Children could identify features that seem to characterize Chandra's collection of poems. They could also compare her work to that of other poets with a similar style to discover what makes these poems unique.

Related Books   Other books of poetry that feature short, vividly descriptive poems:

Chandra, Deborah. *Rich Lizard and Other Poems.*
Harrison, Michael. *Splinters: A Book of Very Short Poems.*
McMillan, Bruce. *One Sun: A Book of Terse Verse.*
Worth, Valerie. *All the Small Poems.*
Worth, Valerie. *Small Poems Again.*

—by Amy McClure and Linda Leonard Lamme

The Best Town in the World

Byrd Baylor. *The Best Town in the World.* Illustrated by
Ronald Himler. New York: Charles Scribner's Sons, 1983.
ISBN 0-684-18035-9.

Suggested Grade Levels: 2–5

Plot Summary

This book is an aesthetic experience, verbally and visually. In poetic prose, Baylor shares with us her father's nostalgic perspective
on his childhood as one of the "Canyon People" in the "best town
in the world." In this town, the people were kinder and friendlier,
the dogs smarter, the summers longer and lovelier, the celebrations
more fun, the swimming hole colder, and the food better than any
other place in the world. Himler's glowing illustrations of starry
nights, beautiful blue skies, and ice-cold swimming holes draw us
completely into that world and make the experiences movingly
believable.

Teaching Suggestions

1. The author writes, "We always liked to hear about that town
   where everything was perfect." Have children try "walking in
   another's shoes" by looking at each picture and discussing why
   the young character might have considered that situation "perfect." Teachers could pose questions such as, If you had been
   that young person, how do you think you would have felt?
   What are your own special memories? What makes these memories special?

2. Teachers could use this book as an introduction to oral history.
   Students could talk with parents, grandparents, or other adults
   in the community. Upper-level students could tape the interviews, put them into written form, and compile a class book of
   oral history. Teachers might encourage students to examine the
   range of special recollections: How are they different? How are
   they the same? How might they have changed over time? The
   class might explore the role nostalgia plays.

3. Students could compare the experiences and settings remembered in this book to contemporary life in their own community. The class might discuss questions such as, What is similar? What is different? What would be the characteristics of "the best town in the world"? In upper grades, students could explore political, social, ecological, and economic issues.

4. Upper-grade students could compare Himler's illustrations to paintings by Norman Rockwell. Teachers might ask about similarities, differences, and the mood of the two sets of pictures.

5. Have students note the elements of humor and exaggeration in Baylor's writing style. Suppose the author's father lived in your town today. Using some of the same stylistic elements that Baylor uses, students could try writing the story of "The Best Town in the World" for their own town (or an imaginary town) as they might remember it in twenty-five years.

Related Books

The following books also feature characters reminiscing about the past:

Ackerman, Karen. *Song and Dance Man.*

Clifford, Eth. *The Remembering Box.*

Cooney, Barbara. *Island Boy.*

Cooney, Barbara. *Miss Rumphius.*

Daly, Niki. *Papa Lucky's Shadow.*

Dragonwagon, Crescent. *Home Place.*

Fox, Mem. *Wilfrid Gordon McDonald Partridge.*

Gerstein, Mordicai. *The Room.*

Greenfield, Eloise. *Honey, I Love, and Other Love Poems.*

Hendershot, Judith. *In Coal Country.*

Hoberman, Mary Ann. *A House Is a House for Me.*

Houston, Gloria. *My Great Aunt Arizona.*

Howard, Elizabeth Fitzgerald. *Aunt Flossie's Hats (and Crab Cakes Later).*

Lasky, Kathryn. *I Have an Aunt on Marlborough Street.*

McCord, David. *Every Time I Climb a Tree.*

McDonald, Megan. *The Potato Man.*

McLerran, Alice. *Roxaboxen.*

Pinkwater, Daniel. *The Big Orange Splot.*

Provensen, Alice, and Martin Provensen. *Shaker Lane.*

Rylant, Cynthia. *The Relatives Came.*
Rylant, Cynthia. *When I Was Young in the Mountains.*
Schecter, Benjamin. *Grandma Remembers.*
Stevenson, James. *Brrr!*

—by Inga Kromann-Kelly

The Book of Pigericks

Arnold Lobel. *The Book of Pigericks*. New York: Harper and Row, 1983. ISBN 0-06-023982-4.

Suggested Grade Levels: 2–7

Plot Summary

Pigericks are limericks about pigs. This collection includes thirty-eight limericks about all kinds of pigs—young pigs, old pigs, warm pigs, cold pigs, stout pigs, smart pigs, light pigs, shy pigs, plain pigs—all in various humorous contexts. There is the "vague pig from Glens Falls who had lost all his windows and walls," "the rude pig from Duluth whose manners were clearly uncouth," and the "old pig in a chair whose cigar brought his wife to despair." Twenty-three limericks place a pig in a particular U.S. city, from such geographically challenging locations as Chanute, Van Nuys, South Goshen, and West Wheeling to the more familiar New York, Key West, and Duluth. Vivid watercolor illustrations bring the porkers and their dilemmas delightfully to life. This is a picture book with appeal and applications far beyond the primary grades.

Teaching Suggestions

1. Teachers could use this book as a geography lesson. Display two large political maps of the United States. Line up two teams, one in front of each map. A reader then recites a pigerick containing the name of a city. When a scorekeeper says "Go!" the first member of each team goes to the team map and locates the city by placing a tack on it. The class can decide on ground rules, such as the number of points awarded for the correct city and state, the number of points that will be awarded to someone who knows only the correct state, and when and how other team members may help.

2. Children can create their own pigericks by coming up with new adjectives to describe a pig, such as *panicky* or *svelte,* and by identifying other U.S. cities.

3. Students could work individually or in groups to create their own book of limerick variations, perhaps a book of "goatericks," "fishericks," or "catericks." They could also illustrate the book and share it with the class.

4. Compare Lobel's pigericks to Edward Lear's limericks. Use globes to play the geography game with Lear's verses, verses such as "There was an old person of Florence," "There was a young lady of Greenwich," or "There was an old man of Calcutta."

5. Have students identify characteristics of limericks by working in groups with two sets of cards. One set has a limerick on each card; the other has a short poem on each card. After reading all of the cards, students sort them into two piles: limericks and non-limericks. Then they can identify characteristics that distinguish limericks from other short poems.

Related Books

Other poetry collections that feature humor and word-play:

Brewton, John E., and Lorraine Blackburn. *They've Discovered a Head in the Box for the Bread and Other Laughable Limericks.*

Brewton, Sara, G. Meredith Blackburn, and John E. Brewton. *My Tang's Tungled and Other Ridiculous Situations: Humorous Poems.*

Clark, Emma Chichester. *I Never Saw a Purple Cow and Other Nonsense Rhymes.*

Hoberman, Mary Ann. *A Fine Fat Pig and Other Animal Poems.*

Jackson, Holbrook. *The Complete Nonsense of Edward Lear.*

Kennedy, X. J., and Dorothy M. Kennedy. *Knock at a Star: A Child's Introduction to Poetry.*

Lear, Edward. *Daffy Down Dillies: Silly Limericks.*

Lewis, Patrick. *A Hippopotamustn't.*

Livingston, Myra Cohn. *A Lollygag of Limericks.*

Merriam, Eve. *Chortles: New and Selected Wordplay Poems.*

—by Inga Kromann-Kelly

Brave Irene

William Steig. *Brave Irene*. New York: Farrar, Straus and Giroux, 1986. ISBN 0-374-30947-7.

Suggested Grade Levels: 1–3

Plot Summary

It was a cold, stormy night when Irene left her warm and cozy house to deliver the ball gown that her sick mother had sewn for the Duchess. On her long and arduous walk over the mountain, poor Irene endures blowing winds, ice, and snow only to watch helplessly when the gown is swept up and away by the strong winds. She finally arrives, breathlessly, at the palace and sees, surprisingly, the gown caught on a tree. Brave Irene proudly reports every detail of her adventurous journey to the impressed and appreciative Duchess.

Readers will linger over Steig's rich use of language, particularly the descriptions and interesting sentence structure (e.g., "Now the wind drove Irene along so rudely she had to hop, skip, and go helter-skeltering over the knobbly ground" and "The wind wrestled her for the package—walloped it, twisted it, shook, snatched at it") and the intriguing comparisons (e.g., "The wind was howling like a wild animal" and "Her good mother who smelled like fresh-baked bread").

Teaching Suggestions

1. Children could discuss experiences of their own when they had to do something adventurous, courageous, or loving.

2. Invite children to create more "Brave Irene" stories. They might also enjoy designing their own illustrations and script for their stories on a roll of paper inserted into a mock television.

3. Discuss the folktale quality of *Brave Irene* and why Irene is a heroine. Students might further discuss the improbable but satisfying ending to this story as another element of its folktale quality.

4. Invite students to talk about Steig's interesting use of language, especially his use of descriptive language and comparisons: "Her good mother who smelled like fresh-baked bread," "How

to get down to that glittering palace," "The wind was howling like a wild animal," "The ball gown flounced out and went waltzing through the powdered air with tissue-paper attendants." Children could also explore the variations of *said* that Steig uses: *admitted, insisted, cautioned, called, snapped, yodeled, shrieked,* and so on. The language in this book offers many opportunities for teachers to create mini-lessons for writing workshops, such as helping students start a chart of the variations of "said" words in this and other books.

Related Books

Other stories about being brave:

Jukes, Mavis. *Like Jake and Me.*

Martin, Bill, Jr., and John Archambault. *The Ghost-Eye Tree.*

Martin, C. L. G. *Three Brave Women.*

Mayhew, James. *Dare You!*

McKissack, Patricia. *Flossie and the Fox.*

Polacco, Patricia. *Thunder Cake.*

Stolz, Mary. *Storm in the Night.*

Zolotow, Charlotte. *The Storm Book.*

Other books by Steig that could be compared to this one:

The Amazing Bone

Amos and Boris

Doctor De Soto

Gorky Rises

Shrek!

Sylvester and the Magic Pebble

—by Janice Kristo and Melissa Keenan

The Cat's Purr

Ashley Bryan. *The Cat's Purr*. New York: Atheneum, 1985.
ISBN 0-689-31086-2.

Suggested Grade Levels: 1–4

Plot Summary

Cat and Rat are very good friends who live side by side and do everything together. Then Cat's uncle presents Cat with a drum. This drum, which only cats are allowed to play, had been passed down in the family for generations. The uncle even teaches Cat how to stroke it so that it will go "purrum purrum." That, of course, is when the trouble begins: Rat wants to play the drum, and Cat won't let him. This conflict leads to a falling out between the two that continues even to this day. In the end, Cat ends up swallowing his drum, but we humans can play it by gently stroking Cat's tummy.

Bryan uses rhythmic and onomatopoeic language in his retelling of this West Indian pourquoi tale. Children will be intrigued by the sounds as they hear Rat's refrain of "Pit-tap-a-la-pat" and "ooo-ooo ooo-ooo." "Uh-huh, uh-huh."

Teaching Suggestions

1. The tale upon which Bryan based *The Cat's Purr* is printed on the last page of the book. Children could compare the original tale to Bryan's version. Then they could find other folktales and write their own versions, to be shared either orally or in written form.

2. This story lends itself to dramatization. Several groups of three could act out the story simultaneously.

3. As you read the story aloud, encourage children to repeat the refrains and to clap or tap the rhythm. Children might enjoy figuring out ways to incorporate various rhythm instruments.

4. Children could compare this story to other pourquoi stories explaining how particular animals acquired certain characteristics (see books listed below by Aardema, Bryan, Dayrell, Goble, Kipling, and Spagnoli). They might also create their own pourquoi tales.

5. Have the children read various versions of *Puss in Boots*. Discuss the ways in which cats are personified. Children might like to try their own personification of a cat or of some other animal.

6. Compare *The Cat's Purr* to Bryan's *The Dancing Granny*. Children might recognize similarities among such elements as the refrains, trickery, and line drawings. A chart comparing these elements could be prepared.

Related Books

Other excellent pourquoi stories:

Aardema, Verna. *Why Mosquitoes Buzz in People's Ears: A West African Tale.*

Arthur, Malcolm. *Puss in Boots.*

Brown, Marcia. *Puss in Boots.*

Bryan, Ashley. *The Dancing Granny.*

Bryan, Ashley. "How Animals Got Their Tails" in *Beat the Story-Drum, Pum-Pum.*

Dayrell, Elphinstone. *Why the Sun and the Moon Live in the Sky: An African Folktale.*

Galdone, Paul. *Puss in Boots.*

Goble, Paul. *Star Boy.*

Kipling, Rudyard. *The Beginning of the Armadillos.*

Kipling, Rudyard. *Just So Stories.*

Larrick, Nancy. *Cats Are Cats.*

Ross, Tony. *Puss in Boots: The Story of a Sneaky Cat.*

Spagnoli, Cathie. *Nine-in-One, Grr! Grr! A Folktale from the Hmong People of Laos.*

Other books on the West Indies:

Bryan, Ashley. *Turtle Knows Your Name.*

Burgie, Irving, and Rosa Guy. *Caribbean Carnival: Songs of the West Indies.*

Sherlock, Philip M. *Anansi, the Spider Man.*

Sherlock, Philip M. *West Indian Folk-tales.*

—by Joan I. Glazer

The Celery Stalks at Midnight

9

James Howe. *The Celery Stalks at Midnight.* Illustrated by Leslie Morrill. New York: Atheneum, 1983. ISBN 0-689-30987-2.

Suggested Grade Levels: 2–5

Plot Summary

This is the third in a series of books written about Harold the dog, Chester the literate cat, Howie the dachshund puppy, and Bunnicula the vampire rabbit, all of whom are owned by the Monroe family. When Chester discovers that Bunnicula is missing from his cage, the cat is certain that the white vegetables lying in the garden and kitchen have been drained of their juices by the vegetarian vampire rabbit. Worse yet, Chester theorizes that in true vampire style, these enslaved vegetables will walk the neighborhoods at night as "killer parsnips, blood-thirsty string beans, and homicidal heads of lettuce." To stop this carnage, the animals set out to spear the vampire veggies with toothpicks, an effort that brings them to an encounter with an ill-tempered white cat and a smelly town dump. Suspense grows when the Monroe boys, Toby and Pete, are seen wearing black capes and behaving in a most alarming fashion. Then Mrs. Monroe is found across town holding a giant white carrot, while Mr. Monroe appears to be drowning in a pool of water amidst a crowd of bystanders. Only after Harold's attempted rescue of his master do the animals learn that these peculiar events are all part of the school carnival. All the while, Bunnicula has been at the carnival in a fancy cage entitled "Castle Bunnicula," on display as Centerville's most unusual pet. In the words of Chester, it was "quite a day."

This unusual, humorous story appeals to a wide range of ages. Additionally, the light, lively style, replete with one outrageous pun after another, makes this an excellent book to stimulate children's awareness of humorous writing.

Teaching Suggestions

1. Children can begin to anticipate the language play and slapstick comedy by discussing the title and the dedication: "To my father, who raised me on corn, ham, and punster cheese." Working in pairs or groups, they could examine each chapter to identify puns and plays-on-words. Discussions might follow about how playing with language functions as an element of humor.

2. Students could list homonyms, rhyming words, and synonyms to make puns and riddles or substitutions in common idioms. Examples from the book can serve as a start. For instance, "What common expression is a withered root vegetable?" Answer: "Dead beet."

3. Bunnicula doesn't appear until close to the end of the story, and then he says nothing. Children could write the school carnival scene from Bunnicula's point of view. They might include dialogue with his agitated animal friends.

4. Students could write a humorous story from their own pet's point of view. Or they could write a story from the point of view of an imaginary pet.

5. Compare this book to the earlier ones, *Bunnicula: A Rabbit Tale of Mystery* and *Howliday Inn*, by having children prepare a chart identifying the main characters, plots, characteristics of the humor, and other elements of style. This could motivate students to read the preceding books as well as encourage a closer look at what constitutes effective sequel-writing.

Related Books

Other books that incorporate humor with animal characters:

Cleary, Beverly. *The Mouse and the Motorcycle.*

Cleary, Beverly. *Ralph S. Mouse.*

Cleary, Beverly. *Runaway Ralph.*

Howe, James. *Bunnicula: A Rabbit Tale of Mystery.*

Howe, James. *Bunnicula: The Vampire Bunny and His Friends.*

Howe, James. *Howliday Inn.*

Howe, James. *Return to Howliday Inn.*

Kennedy, Richard. *Song of the Horse.*

King-Smith, Dick. *Ace: The Very Important Pig.*

King-Smith, Dick. *Babe: The Gallant Pig.*

King-Smith, Dick. *Pigs Might Fly.*

Lawson, Robert. *Ben and Me.*

Lawson, Robert. *Mr. Revere and I.*
Meddaugh, Susan. *Martha Speaks.*
Scieszka, Jon. *The Frog Prince, Continued.*
Scieszka, Jon. *The True Story of the Three Little Pigs.*
Selden, George. *The Cricket in Times Square.*
Stolz, Mary. *Quentin Pig.*
Talbott, Hudson. *We're Back! A Dinosaur's Story.*
Yolen, Jane. *Commander Toad and the Dis-Asteroid.*
Yolen, Jane. *Piggins.*

—by Inga Kromann-Kelly

Chicka Chicka Boom Boom

Bill Martin, Jr., and John Archambault. *Chicka Chicka Boom Boom*. Illustrated by Lois Ehlert. New York: Simon and Schuster, 1989. ISBN 0-671-67949-X.

Suggested Grade Levels: Preschool–1

Plot Summary

"A told B, and B told C, 'I'll meet you at the top of the coconut tree.'" Thus begins this unique rhythmic alphabet book, one reminiscent of a children's playground chant. All the little lower-case letters scramble to the top of the coconut tree. But the question is, "Chicka chicka boom boom! Will there be enough room?" When Z arrives, the tree topples and all the big upper-case letters come to the rescue. One by one in alphabetical order the disheveled letters emerge from the pile-up. Each is slightly the worse for wear: "skinned-knee D and stubbed-toe E and patched-up F . . ." The sun goes down behind the coconut tree, but a full moon comes up and—"Dare double dare, you can't catch me"—A is back climbing the coconut tree.

This book invites a lot of talk and language play from young children. After only one reading youngsters were heard repeating lines and making up some of their own. Each page is framed with a polka-dot patterned border in shocking pink and orange, making the book unusually inviting and appealing.

Teaching Suggestions

1. Children often notice each letter as it arrives at the coconut tree and enjoy hunting for particular letters in the pile-up.

2. Children also enjoy speculating about whether all the letters will follow A back up the coconut tree. Children have theorized that some letters won't go back up the tree because "they got hurt too much—like 'black-eyed P'."

3. Encourage group chanting and dramatization as the book is reread aloud.

4. Compare this book to Bill Martin's other stories and poems, particularly those from his *Sounds of Language* series.

5. Children could be encouraged to create their own story using the alphabet as an organizing framework.

6. Children could decorate an oversized letter and create accompanying adventures.

7. Read a range of alphabet books aloud and explore the similarities and differences among them.

Related Books

Other alphabet books with a rhymed or alliterative text:

Base, Graeme. *Animalia.*

Brown, Marcia. *All Butterflies: An ABC.*

Dragonwagon, Crescent. *Alligator Arrived with Apples: A Potluck Alphabet Feast.*

Ehlert, Lois. *Eating the Alphabet: Fruits and Vegetables from A to Z.*

Lobel, Anita. *Alison's Zinnia.*

Purviance, Susan, and Marcia O'Shell. *Alphabet Annie Announces an All-American Album.*

Sendak, Maurice. *Alligators All Around.*

—by Carol Avery

Dear Mr. Henshaw

Beverly Cleary. *Dear Mr. Henshaw.* Illustrated by Paul O. Zelinsky. New York: William Morrow, 1983. ISBN 0-688-02405-X.

Suggested Grade Levels: 3–7

Plot Summary

Leigh Botts begins writing to his favorite author, Mr. Henshaw, in second grade and continues throughout his grade school years, eventually turning to journal writing. Through his writing, Leigh reveals anxieties such as being the new boy in school, frustrations over his parents' divorce and estrangement from his father, concerns about the family dog Bandit ("Mom got me and Dad got Bandit"), and thoughts about the general ups and downs of growing up. Mr. Henshaw's actual correspondence is never revealed; nevertheless, he clearly plays an important role in the young boy's life. Readers of this book learn not only about coping with life, but also about the rewards and difficulties writers face. The author of this Newbery award–winning book captures the voice of young Leigh Botts with candor, compassion, and humor.

Teaching Suggestions

1. Mr. Henshaw asks Leigh to answer ten questions about himself. Children could respond to these same ten questions by writing about themselves and comparing their lives to Leigh's.

2. One of Leigh's satisfactions is that he gets special treats in his school lunchbag because his mother works for a catering service. Unfortunately, the treats are regularly stolen. Finally, Leigh invents a burglar alarm that not only solves his lunch problems, but makes him something of a hero to his classmates as well. This episode can be a springboard for considering inventions and how they come about. Children could work in groups to replicate Leigh's invention and discuss whether it would really work. Or they could present other innovative ways to catch the lunchbag thief. They might also try to create inventions to solve their own classroom problems.

3. Through their son's writing, Leigh's mother and father emerge as believable characters. Students can learn about characterization by writing a thumbnail sketch of Leigh's parents and then

sharing their perceptions with each other. They can also consider how an author brings a character to life by identifying episodes in the story that contribute to characterization. Or students could write a thumbnail sketch describing someone in their own family. The class could then discuss how the information from such a sketch might be included in a story.

4. Children can be motivated to do many kinds of letter and journal writing after reading this book, including letters to favorite authors about their books, letter exchanges with other classes near and far, journal writing in general, and journal writing in connection with specific activities.

5. This book can also stimulate middle- and upper-level students to learn more about authors and authorship. How did their favorite authors get started writing? What do they have to say about writing for young people? In addition to requesting author material from publishers, students could use reference sources for biographical information and read journal articles by and about the authors they've decided to study. Students might then like to start an author file in the classroom or school library.

6. Cleary wrote a sequel to *Dear Mr. Henshaw.* Students could speculate about what happens in this sequel. Encourage them to think about features of the story and about what characters and settings might continue or be added. This would be an excellent lead-in to the actual sequel, *Strider.*

Related Books

The following books also use a journal format:

Avi. *The True Confessions of Charlotte Doyle.*

Blos, Joan W. *A Gathering of Days: A New England Girl's Journal, 1830–32.*

Byars, Betsy. *The Burning Questions of Bingo Brown.*

Farber, Norma. *Mercy Short: A Winter Journal, North Boston, 1692–93.*

Harvey, Brett. *Cassie's Journey: Going West in the 1860's.*

Little, Jean. *Hey World, Here I Am!*

Mazer, Norma. *I, Trissy.*

Paulsen, Gary. *The Island.*

Turner, Ann. *Nettie's Trip South.*

Books focusing on the topic of divorce:

Blume, Judy. *It's Not the End of the World.*

Byars, Betsy. *The Animal, the Vegetable, and John D. Jones.*

Cleary, Beverly. *Strider.*

Danziger, Paula. *The Divorce Express.*

Fine, Anne. *My War with Goggle-Eyes.*

Janeczko, Paul B. *Strings: A Gathering of Family Poems.*

Livingston, Myra Cohn. *There Was a Place and Other Poems.*

Myers, Walter Dean. *The Mouse Rap.*

If children want to read more about inventions, they could examine the following books:

Lambert, David, and Jane Insley. *Great Discoveries and Inventions.*

Lasson, Kenneth. *Mousetraps and Muffling Cups: One Hundred Brilliant and Bizarre United States Patents.*

—by Inga Kromann-Kelly

12 The Dove's Letter

Keith Baker. *The Dove's Letter.* San Diego: Harcourt Brace Jovanovich, 1988. ISBN 0-15-224133-7.

Suggested Grade Levels: 3–6

Plot Summary

When a dove finds a beautifully written letter whose message she cannot read, she embarks on a journey to find the very special person for whom the letter is intended. In her travels, the dove discovers that the meaning of the words changes depending on the recipient. The letter's final destination gives hope to a soldier who has been in battle for many years and has lost his zest for life. Repetitive elements in both the story and the illustrations emphasize the universal need of individuals to love and be loved in return. Baker's story gently asserts the power that words have in our search to connect with others.

Teaching Suggestions

1. Provide students with a short paragraph that might be interpreted differently depending on the reader. Also provide them with an accompanying list of character descriptions. (Students could also be challenged to write their own paragraph and list of characters.) Using the two items, discuss how words may be interpreted differently depending on who is doing the reading. How might one character from the list interpret the paragraph differently from another? Emphasize the concept of interaction between reader and text.

2. Baker uses repetition in describing the dove's journey and onomatopoeia in describing the activities of the characters in the book. Discuss the way in which both techniques enhance the text. Invite children to incorporate these literary devices in their own writing.

3. Using this book on Valentine's Day, discuss various ways of expressing love for people, animals, stuffed animals, etc. through language. Examples might include songs, poetry, letters, and conversations. Ask the students to plan original messages to be delivered to the person of their choice on February 14.

4. The book ends with the soldier ready to deliver the letter to a love of long ago. Ask several pairs of students to role-play what occurs as the letter is delivered and what happens afterward.

Related Books

Other books that use letters as a focus:

Ahlberg, Janet, and Allan Ahlberg. *The Jolly Postman; or, Other People's Letters.*
Brisson, Pat. *Your Best Friend, Kate.*
Brisson, Pat. *Kate Heads West.*
Cleary, Beverly. *Dear Mr. Henshaw.*
James, Simon. *Dear Mr. Blueberry.*
Keats, Ezra Jack. *A Letter to Amy.*
Legum, Margaret. *Mailbox, Quailbox.*

Books about Valentine's Day and sending Valentines:

Cohen, Barbara. *Two Hundred Thirteen Valentines.*
dePaola, Tomie. *Things to Make and Do for Valentine's Day.*
Geringer, Laura. *Yours 'til the Ice Cracks: A Book of Valentines.*
Modell, Frank. *One Zillion Valentines.*
Prelutsky, Jack. *It's Valentine's Day.*
Wittman, Sally. *The Boy Who Hated Valentine's Day.*

Also see the extensive list of related books for *The Jolly Postman; or, Other People's Letters* by Janet and Allan Ahlberg.

—by Cheryl Grossman

The Eleventh Hour: A Curious Mystery

Graeme Base. *The Eleventh Hour: A Curious Mystery*. New York: Harry N. Abrams, 1989. ISBN 0-8109-0851-4.

Suggested Grade Levels: 3–8

Plot Summary

Who stole the feast? Filled with bold, glossy illustrations, this book brims with mystery and riddles to be solved. Horace, an elephant, decides to throw an elaborate birthday party for himself as he turns eleven. Thus, everything in this book happens in elevens: eleven kinds of food, eleven games to play, eleven animals at the party. One of the guests, however, steals Horace's magnificent feast. The reader must follow various trails of clues in order to find the thief. Names are cleverly camouflaged, and clues are hidden in hedges, borders, buttons, mirrors, and stained glass windows. The solution can only be found in a sealed packet at the end of the book, challenging readers to solve the mystery on their own.

Base's artwork depicts unique, overhead perspectives such as animals lounging on Persian carpets while playing chutes and ladders, a swan sitting on a chair while playing cards, and a Bengal tiger leaping in the air to catch a ball during a cricket match. The punk zebra is a particularly imaginative touch.

Teaching Suggestions

1. Small groups could closely examine the book together and try to solve the mystery. An ongoing class chart of the clues discovered by each group could be compiled.

2. Children might like to write their own mysteries and challenge classmates to solve them.

3. Have children examine Base's artwork and compare it to the artwork in his other books. They could also compare Base to famous artists who work in a similar style in order to draw conclusions about him as an artist.

4. Share George Shannon's *Stories to Solve,* Ann Jonas's *Thirteenth Clue,* and David Macaulay's *Black and White,* all of which have a similar guessing game format.

Related Books   Other mysteries that could be read along with this book:

Giff, Patricia Reilly. *Polka Dot Private Eye.*

Howe, James. The *Sebastian Barth* series.

Joosse, Barbara M. *Wild Willie and King Kyle: Detectives.*

Raskin, Ellen. *The Westing Game.*

Simon, Seymour. The *Einstein Anderson* series.

Sobol, Donald. The *Encyclopedia Brown* series.

Williams, Kit. *Masquerade.*

Other books by Base that could be compared to this one include *Animalia* and *Jabberwocky.*

—by Susan Lehr

Feathers for Lunch

Lois Ehlert. *Feathers for Lunch*. San Diego: Harcourt Brace Jovanovich, 1990. ISBN 0-15-230550-5.

Suggested Grade Levels: Preschool–3

Plot Summary

The door's been left open a crack, and the cat has escaped to find a tasty bird for lunch. He goes after ten different birds, but all he catches are "feathers for lunch."

This tale is cleverly told through verse and brilliant collage paintings. A different species of bird appears on each page. Some pages also have different species of plants. Both the birds and the plants are accurately drawn and labeled. Some of the birds also have their "song" transcribed into words (e.g., "what, cheer, cheer, cheer" for the cardinal). In addition, the words "Jingle, Jingle" are found on each page to signal the approach of the cat.

The last four pages of the book present "the lunch that got away." Here Ehlert has painted each bird and listed basic information: size, food, where the bird nests, and the area of the country in which the bird can be found. A note on the final page reads, "All birds illustrated in this book, excluding those on the last four pages, are portrayed life size." This note leads readers back to the text to compare the house wren to the red-headed woodpecker or the ruby-throated hummingbird to the northern oriole. Even the flap of the book jacket is meant to be read by young readers. Here Ehlert lists all the birds with a box for checking answers and asks, "How many of these birds can you find in your area?"

Teaching Suggestions

1. The large print, the labels on the pictures, and the rhyme scheme provide support for beginning readers. Encourage children to find the "Jingle, Jingle" on each page, to talk about the rhyme, and to closely examine the birds and plants.

2. This book is a fine example of a multi-genre piece of literature; both poetry and informational formats are included. Thus, it can be a useful model for showing children the ways in which writers can present information in interesting formats to entice readers. A teacher might present this book as one example of

writing that breaks away from traditional report writing. (Also see Ehlert's *Making Vegetable Soup,* which has a similar format but focuses on unusual vegetables.)

3. Children could create their own guidebook for bird-watching (or other animal-watching) in their area using this book as a model.

4. In both format and illustration, this book invites comparison to some of the books by Eric Carle. Discuss collage illustrations and offer children the opportunity to experiment with this technique. Children might also compare this book to Ehlert's *Making Vegetable Soup.*

Related Books

The following are other good books about birds and observing nature:

Brown, Mary Barrett. *Wings along the Waterway.*

Fleischman, Paul. *I Am Phoenix: Poems for Two Voices.*

Livingston, Myra Cohn. *If the Owl Calls Again: A Collection of Owl Poems.*

Parnall, Peter. *Quiet.*

Patent, Dorothy Hinshaw. *Feathers.*

Reid, Struan. *Bird World.*

Rockwell, Anne. *Our Yard Is Full of Birds.*

Singer, Marilyn. *Turtle in July.*

Smith, William Jay. *Birds and Beasts.*

Tyrrell, Ester Q. *Hummingbirds: Jewels of the Sky.*

Yolen, Jane. *Bird Watch: A Book of Poetry.*

The Very Hungry Caterpillar, The Very Busy Spider, and *The Grouchy Ladybug,* all by Eric Carle, are excellent books to compare with this one.

Another similar book by Ehlert is *Making Vegetable Soup.*

—by Carol Avery

15 Flossie and the Fox

Patricia McKissack. *Flossie and the Fox*. Illustrated by Rachel Isadora. New York: Dial Books, 1986. ISBN 0-8037-0250-7.

Suggested Grade Levels: 1–3

Plot Summary

When Big Mama asks Flossie to take a basket of fresh eggs over to Miz Viola, she warns her to be careful. A clever old fox, it seems, keeps stealing the eggs by managing to outwit the hounds. On the way to Miz Viola's, Flossie meets the fox. He tries to scare her by tirelessly attempting to convince her that he is indeed who he says he is, boasting that he has a fox's fur and a bushy tail. In an effort to outwit the fox, however, Flossie remains unconvinced. And when Flossie safely reaches Miz Viola's, she sends the hounds after the not-so-clever fox.

McKissack's language captures the beauty of the dialect with sentences such as "I disremember ever seeing one, chile, that rascal." Clues about the time and setting of the story are imparted to readers through specific words and phrases, such as *smokehouse, Sophie's Quarters,* and *cabins.* The rhythmic language begs to be read aloud and appreciated again and again.

Teaching Suggestions

1. This book is wonderful to share aloud because of the dialect and the beautiful rhythmic cadence of the language. Children might come to appreciate the language even more by creating a Readers Theatre or by acting out scenes using puppets.

2. Help students explore how spellings and grammar are changed to convey dialect. Examples from the story include "She say, Seem like they been troubled"; "he so scared"; "Why come, that 'ol slicker, I tell you"; How do a fox look?"; "I disremember ever seeing one, chile, that rascal"; and "Don't tarry now. Yes'um."

3. Ask why Flossie was so successful in outwitting the fox. Did the fox deserve what happened to him at the end?

4. Flossie is such a brave and clever character. Students might enjoy creating additional "Flossie" adventures.

5. Discuss McKissack's introduction to this story with the children. She writes about the impact of listening to family stories. Students might share some of their own family stories and use these as possible topics for writing.

6. Discuss McKissack's clues to the time and setting of the story, such as her use of language (e.g., cabins, Sophie's Quarters, smokehouse, chicken coop, hollow log), props (e.g., straw doll, basket of fresh eggs, fox, chickens), and actions (e.g., wrapped her hands and face with her apron, clicked her teeth and shook her head, putting a peach in her apron pocket).

Related Books

Other picture books that feature a brave heroine who outwits another character:

Browne, Anthony. *Willy the Wimp.*

Glen, Maggie. *Ruby.*

McKissack, Patricia. *Mirandy and Brother Wind.*

Steig, William. *Brave Irene.*

Trickster tales:

Aardema, Verna. *Bimwili and the Zimwi: A Tale from Zanzibar.*

Bang, Molly. *Wiley and the Hairy Man: Adapted from an American Folk Tale.*

dePaola, Tomie. *Fin M'Coul: The Giant of Knockmany Hill.*

Goble, Paul. *Iktomi and the Ducks: A Plains Indian Story.*

Jones, Hettie. *Coyote Tales.*

Lester, Julius. *The Knee-High Man and Other Tales.*

Morimoto, Junko. *The Inch Boy.*

Muller, Robin. *Mollie Whuppie and the Giant.*

Young, Ed. *The Terrible Nung Gwama: A Chinese Folktale.*

For a related title about outsmarting a fox, see James Marshall's *Fox Outfoxed.*

—by Janice Kristo and Melissa Keenan

16 Foolish Rabbit's Big Mistake

Rafe Martin. *Foolish Rabbit's Big Mistake.* Illustrated by Ed Young. New York: G. P. Putnam's Sons, 1985. ISBN 0-399-21178-0.

Suggested Grade Levels: K–3

Plot Summary

In the early morning, before he is fully awake, little Rabbit begins wondering what would happen if the earth broke up. Just then he hears a loud crash. Terrified, he begins running wildly, spreading the news that the earth is, in fact, breaking up. All the other animals also panic, except Lion, who forces Rabbit to return to the place where he heard the crash. Rabbit must then tell the others that it was only an apple falling to the ground. The animals' anger at Rabbit is cut short by Lion, however, who reminds them that they too ran without knowing what was frightening them.

This Indian Jataka tale has a cumulative structure and retains the rhythmic quality of stories in the oral tradition. The illustrations are magnificent, with a full, double-page spread of the lion's paw as Rabbit sees it followed by a full, double-page spread of the lion's face that will cause audiences of young children to gasp.

Teaching Suggestions

1. Explore the theme of investigating fear rather than running from it. Have children suggest actual incidents where this theme applies, either in their own lives or in books they have read.

2. Children could compare this story to versions of *Chicken Little* or *Henny Penny.* A class chart detailing similarities and differences in plot structure, character reactions to the main event, and other elements could be created.

3. Invite children to role-play alternative solutions to Rabbit's problem or alternative actions by the animals.

4. Have children take the role of Rabbit or one of the other animals and tell how they felt when they first saw Lion.

5. The cumulative structure of Martin's book could be explored and compared to the structure of books such as Kent's *The Fat Cat,* Tanaka's *The Chase,* Hogrogian's *The Cat Who Loved to Sing,* and Wood's *The Napping House* and *King Bidgood's in the Bathtub.* Encourage children to create their own stories with a cumulative structure.

Related Books

Other books with a cumulative story structure:

Bishop, Gavin. *Chicken Licken.*

Galdone, Paul. *Henny Penny.*

Hogrogian, Nonny. *The Cat Who Loved to Sing.*

Kellogg, Steven. *Chicken Little.*

Kent, Jack. *The Fat Cat: A Danish Folktale.*

Tanaka, Beatrice. *The Chase: A Retelling of a Kutenai Indian Tale.*

Wood, Audrey. *King Bidgood's in the Bathtub.*

Wood, Audrey. *The Napping House.*

Zimmermann, H. Werner. *Henny Penny.*

Trickster tales:

Aardema, Verna. *Tales from the Story Hat.*

Bang, Molly. *Wiley and the Hairy Man: Adapted from an American Folk Tale.*

McKissack, Patricia. *Flossie and the Fox.*

Also see the list of related books for *Heckedy Peg* and *Little Tricker the Squirrel Meets Big Double the Bear.*

—by Joan I. Glazer

Frank and Ernest

Alexandra Day. *Frank and Ernest.* New York: Scholastic, 1988.
ISBN 0-590-41557-3.

Suggested Grade Levels: 3–5

Plot Summary

Frank and Ernest, an enterprising bear and elephant, place an ad in the yellow pages offering to care for a small business or store while the owner is away. They are hired by Mrs. Miller, who leaves them in charge of a diner. Frank and Ernest do an admirable job after learning the occupational dialect. Children will delight in hearing the simple orders of customers translated into creative phrases as the orders are passed on to the chef. Next time you want a hamburger with lettuce, tomato, and onion, why don't you just say "burn one, take it through the garden, and pin a rose on it"? Day's realistic illustrations humorously convey both a day's work at the diner as well as the cooperation and friendship between Frank and Ernest. A glossary of restaurant jargon adds to the appeal of this book.

Teaching Suggestions

1. Have children create diner language descriptions for foods not mentioned in the book. Illustrations could be drawn and displayed along with the creative and actual names of the foods chosen.

2. Invite parents and others who use occupational dialects to talk to the class about their special language. Have the visitors discuss the meaning of the words used. Students could then further explore the origins of these words and phrases.

3. Ask the children how their dialect differs from that of their older siblings or parents. Have the children interview their parents and ask about words that either were used in their parents' youth that are not in use today or whose meanings have changed. Compile a class list to indicate differences in dialect and how language changes over time.

4. Using the glossary, recite the diner description of a given food. Have the children guess what is being described and give a rationale for their guess.

Related Books The following books also focus on idioms related to particular occupations or pastimes:

Day, Alexandra. *Frank and Ernest Play Ball.*

Terban, Marvin. *Mad as a Wet Hen! and Other Funny Idioms.*

For a related title about finding jobs, see *Jobs for Kids: The Guide to Having Fun and Making Money* by Carol Barkin and Elizabeth James.

—by Cheryl Grossman

Galimoto

Karen Lynn Williams. *Galimoto*. Illustrated by Catherine Stock.
New York: Lothrop, Lee and Shepard, 1990. ISBN 0-688-08789-2.

Suggested Grade Levels: K–3

Plot Summary

Galimoto means *car* in Chichewa, the national language of Malawi, a nation in southeast Africa. It is also the name for a type of push-toy made by Malawian children from old wires, sticks, or corn-stalks. Kondi, a boy of seven, wants to make a galimoto, but he has only scraps of wire. In the course of trading a knife, begging from his uncle, and resourcefully tapping several other means, Kondi gathers enough wire to make his galimoto. It will be a pickup truck to carry maize to the city. Kondi works all afternoon to make his galimoto from the wire, using a large stick of bamboo as the steering column. That evening, after supper, Kondi glides his galimoto over the dusty path in the moonlight. His friends form a line behind him, chanting to cheer his accomplishment.

Williams taught hearing-impaired students in Malawi. This story is drawn from her experiences with the village children and thus accurately reflects the flavor of life in this African country. Stock's luminous, detailed watercolors add to the realism.

Teaching Suggestions

1. Read the book aloud and invite children's responses. Teachers may want to locate Malawi on a globe for young children. Children might also appreciate learning about how the author gathered information to write the story.

2. Children could discuss their favorite toys or ideas for making toys. They could also compare their playthings to those of Kondi.

3. The illustrations in this book greatly enhance the story. Text and pictures can lead to appreciation of another culture. Children could consider the differences between Kondi's village and their own towns, cities, and homes and then create a comparison/contrast chart.

4. Compare this book to other picture books about Africa and create a web of images and associations children have developed from reading these books. These new images could be compared to the prejudices or misconceptions they might have had before reading.

Related Books

Other picture books focusing on African experiences:

Isadora, Rachel. *At the Crossroads.*

Schermbrucker, Reviva. *Charlie's House.*

Stanley, Sanna. *The Rains Are Coming.*

Williams, Karen Lynn. *When Africa Was Home.*

For a related book about making African crafts, see Judith Hoffman Corwin's *African Crafts.*

—by Linda Leonard Lamme

The Ghost-Eye Tree

Bill Martin, Jr., and John Archambault. *The Ghost-Eye Tree.*
Illustrated by Ted Rand. New York: Henry Holt, 1985.
ISBN 0-8050-0208-1.

Suggested Grade Levels: K–2

Plot Summary

It is a dark and windy autumn night when a young boy and his sister are sent to the end of town to get a bucket of milk. Along the way, the two manage to get past the ghostly old oak tree—the halfway tree. On their return, however, the boy hears something and the ghost-eye tree seems to reach for him. Both children run for home, spilling milk as they go. Once safely outside their home, both admit they were afraid. Still, when the boy realizes that he has lost the hat that makes him feel "tough," a hat his sister has said makes him look "stupid," it is she who dashes back after it.

The repetition and lyrical quality of the text make this an excellent book to read aloud. Reading aloud serves to heighten the suspense as well. The illustrations build up both the spooky quality of the story and the humor.

Teaching Suggestions

1. After hearing the story read aloud, children could pantomime the trip to town. Appropriate music could be selected to accompany their walk, or perhaps part of the class could make sound effects.

2. Children could create a mural or story map showing the house, the path, the tree, and Mr. Cowlander's barn. Using this mural or map, the children could then retell the story using stick characters or puppets.

3. After noting the elements that make this story so suspenseful, children could write their own haunting tales. The children might be encouraged to consider a time when they were frightened and to embellish on this event when creating their own tales. These tales could be shared orally with the class and accompanied by spooky music.

4. Children could create a web of ways to overcome fear. They could then compare their ways to those used by the children in the story.

5. Children could compare the adventures described in this book to those experienced by children in similar stories (see the list below).

Related Books

Other books that explore night fears:

Bunting, Eve. *Ghost's Hour, Spook's Hour.*

Fox, Mem. *Night Noises.*

Grifalconi, Ann. *Darkness and the Butterfly.*

Stolz, Mary. *Storm in the Night.*

Williams, Linda. *The Little Old Lady Who Was Not Afraid of Anything.*

Winthrop, Elizabeth. *Tough Eddie.*

Related books about overcoming fears:

Martin, C. L. G. *Three Brave Women.*

Mayhew, James. *Dare You!*

Polacco, Patricia. *Thunder Cake.*

Steig, William. *Brave Irene.*

Collections of poems about the night:

Fox, Siv Cedering. *The Blue Horse and Other Night Poems.*

Hill, Helen, Agnes Perkins, Anne Burgess, and Alethea Helbig. *Dusk to Dawn: Poems of Night.*

Larrick, Nancy. *When the Dark Comes Dancing: A Bedtime Poetry Book.*

—by Joan I. Glazer

The Green Lion of Zion Street

Julia Fields. *The Green Lion of Zion Street.* Illustrated by Jerry Pinkney. New York: Margaret K. McElderry Books, 1988. ISBN 0-689-50414-4.

Suggested Grade Levels: K–6

Plot Summary

"Right in the city / in a certain place / a beast is crouched / with a scowl on its face"—the green lion of Zion Street. Julia Fields impressionistically offers this repetitive and rhythmic narrative about a group of urban children waiting while "the bus be's late / . . . in weather ten times colder / than a roller skate." Fields uses the voice of one of these children to describe the imaginative caper of the stone lion statue in the park, which has come alive and is about to attack: "They think that it will roar out loud . . . / Its jaws are declarative and wide / You see a mane / and, next, one paw / and then another / and . . . O Brother!" Pinkney's deft use of line and color in the pencil and watercolor illustrations convey movement and energy.

Teaching Suggestions

1. Students can increase their interest in the poetic nature of this book through choral speaking.

2. Students can reenact the imaginary experience of the narrative through the use of creative dramatization. Pantomime, dialogue, movement, and costumes lend themselves well as students consider what happened on Zion Street and dramatize the situations described in the poem.

3. Students could share times when they pretended (or when they believed) something was real, describing how they reacted to it.

4. Compare the language, mood, and tone in this book to that of the poems in *On City Streets* by Nancy Larrick or *A Song in Stone* by Lee Bennett Hopkins.

Related Books   Other books about children living in urban settings:

Adoff, Arnold. *City in All Directions: An Anthology of Modern Poems.*

Greenfield, Eloise. *Night on Neighborhood Street.*

Hopkins, Lee Bennett. *A Song in Stone: City Poems.*

Larrick, Nancy. *On City Streets: An Anthology of Poetry.*

Lenski, Lois. *Sing a Song of People.*

Turner, Ann. *Street Talk.*

—by Darwin L. Henderson

Halloween ABC

Eve Merriam. *Halloween ABC*. Illustrated by Lane Smith.
New York: Macmillan, 1987. ISBN 0-02-766870-3.

Plot Summary

Twenty-six Halloween poems, one for each letter of the alphabet, make up this delightfully chilling collection. Children will shiver as they listen to the truly frightening and eerie poetry. Each poem is more gruesome than the next. Yet the visual imagery is intended to create a playful sort of horror. For example, apples are "delicious, malicious; but one bite and you're dead," and creepy crawlers are "crawling down your throat / into your gizzard / where they float, float, float." Merriam obviously enjoys playing with sound in her poetry, using internal rhymes such as "lunging, plunging" and creating alliterative lines like "virulent, villain, venomous, vile." Many of the poems also have a cadence that beckons the listener to move rhythmically as the poem is read. A warning for those who dare to read these poems: "Shiver and tremble and don't dare shriek; the creatures can tell / if you're faint or weak."

Teaching Suggestions

1. The poetry in this book is rich in vivid imagery and descriptive action. Many of the poems thus lend themselves to dramatic and rhythmic interpretation. Selections such as "Crawlers" and "Lair" could be choreographed and presented in dance form or used as a stimulus for dramatic interpretation.

2. Compare these poems to those in Jack Prelutsky's *Nightmares: Poems to Trouble Your Sleep* and *The Headless Horseman Rides Tonight: More Poems to Trouble Your Sleep.* A discussion focusing on the elements in the poetry that help to create a frightened response could motivate children to write their own scary poetry or even attempt a horror story.

3. One of the poems is titled "Xylophone." Give the children rhythm instruments such as sticks, bells, cymbals, and drums. Encourage them to write frightening poetry about their instrument. A poetry reading with rhythm instrument accompaniment could follow.

4. Many fiendish characters are depicted in Merriam's poetry. After discussing the physical qualities and personality traits that contribute to their fiendish nature, invite the children to create monster-gargoyles or demon-crawlers from self-hardening clay. Once completed, children could give their character "voice" by writing and presenting an appropriate monologue for the sculpture.

Related Books

Other good poetry and short story collections on the theme of Halloween:

Bauer, Caroline Feller. *Halloween: Stories and Poems.*

Brewton, John E., Lorraine A. Blackburn, and G. Meredith Blackburn. *In the Witch's Kitchen: Poems for Halloween.*

Bunting, Eve. *Scary, Scary Halloween.*

Cecil, Laura. *Boo! Stories to Make You Jump.*

Hopkins, Lee Bennett. *Creatures: Poems.*

Livingston, Myra Cohn. *Halloween Poems.*

McKissack, Patricia. *The Dark Thirty: Southern Tales of the Supernatural.*

Prelutsky, Jack. *Nightmares: Poems to Trouble Your Sleep.*

Prelutsky, Jack. *The Headless Horseman Rides Tonight: More Poems to Trouble Your Sleep.*

Riley, James Whitcomb. *Little Orphant Annie.*

Schwartz, Alvin. *Scary Stories to Tell in the Dark.*

Schwartz, Alvin. *More Scary Stories to Tell in the Dark.*

Schwartz, Alvin. *Scary Stories 3: More Tales to Chill Your Bones.*

—by Cheryl Grossman

Heartland

Diane Siebert. *Heartland.* With paintings by Wendell Minor. New York: Thomas Y. Crowell, 1989. ISBN 0-690-04730-4.

Suggested Grade Levels: 2–8

Plot Summary

This book is a perfect blend of colorful, full-page paintings and an original poem about farming in the Midwest, our nation's heartland. While the content of the poem is more appropriate for older children, the illustrations and poetic language will keep all ages spellbound. Farmlands are created "square by square—A quilt of life I proudly wear." The farmer has a feed-and-seed cap to shield his weathered face, "A face whose every crease and line can tell a tale." "I am the Heartland," the poem repeats, "I survive to keep America, my home, alive."

Teaching Suggestions

1. This moving book prompts children to consider rural life and how working the land promotes use of the senses. Writing poems about their own individual heartlands would be a natural extension, as would painting landscapes. In one class, children studied the personification in the poem and wrote poems with titles such as "I am the soccer field," "I am the waterfall," and "I am the city park."

2. This book's content is rich with descriptions of farmland, making it ideal for historical studies of our nation's agricultural heartland as well as geographic studies of the Midwest. Students will develop a greater appreciation for their social studies content when poetry is part of the curriculum. Children could make a collage of images of rural America (or other landscapes) using symbols from the book, such as a windmill, a silo, or a DeKalb Corn sign.

3. Have children make a list of descriptive words used in the poem and discuss how these words heighten the poem's meaning.

4. Invite children to select their favorite parts of the book and, working in small groups, create Readers Theatre presentations.

5. Children could also examine other picture book versions of well-known poems, such as some of the books listed below, to see how illustrations can affect a reader's perception of the text.

Related Books

Other books that feature a single poem in picture book format:

Baylor, Byrd. *Hawk, I'm Your Brother.*

Carroll, Lewis. *Jabberwocky.* Illustrated by Graeme Base.

Eliot, T. S. *Growltiger's Last Stand.* Illustrated by Errol Le Cain.

Frost, Robert. *Birches.* Illustrated by Ed Young.

Frost, Robert. *Stopping by Woods on a Snowy Evening.* Illustrated by Susan Jeffers.

Lear, Edward. *The Owl and the Pussycat.* Illustrated by Janet Stevens.

Lewis, Richard. *In the Night, Still Dark.* Illustrated by Ed Young.

Longfellow, Henry Wadsworth. *Hiawatha.* Illustrated by Susan Jeffers.

Longfellow, Henry Wadsworth. *Paul Revere's Ride.* Illustrated by Ted Rand.

Mayer, Mercer. *The Pied Piper of Hamelin.*

Noyes, Alfred. *The Highwayman.* Illustrated by Charles Mikolaycak.

Riley, James Whitcomb. *Little Orphant Annie.* Illustrated by Diane Stanley.

Service, Robert. *The Shooting of Dan McGrew.* Illustrated by Ted Harris.

Siebert, Diane. *Mojave.*

Siebert, Diane. *Plane Song.*

Siebert, Diane. *Train Song.*

Thayer, Ernest Lawrence. *Casey at the Bat.* Illustrated by Wallace Tripp.

Willard, Nancy. *A Visit to William Blake's Inn.*

—by Linda Leonard Lamme

23 Heckedy Peg

Audrey Wood. *Heckedy Peg.* Illustrated by Don Wood. San Diego: Harcourt Brace Jovanovich, 1987. ISBN 0-15-233678-8.

Suggested Grade Levels: 1–4

Plot Summary

Before setting off to market, a poor, loving mother asks each of her seven children, named for the days of the week, what they would like her to bring home. Warning the children not to let strangers in and not to play with fire, the mother leaves. The children, however, are tricked into disobeying their mother by a witch named Heckedy Peg, who subsequently uses a spell to turn the children into a delectable feast for her own enjoyment. It takes quite a bit of cunning and the mother's devotion to her children to break the spell and engineer the demise of the witch.

Although a contemporary story, Heckedy Peg follows the form of traditional folktales. Common elements include trickery, magic spells, chants, and the triumph of good over evil, leading, of course, to the ever-present happy ending. Richly detailed oil paintings contrast the warmth of home with the dark, ominous witch's hut and combine with the text to create a timeless story.

Teaching Suggestions

1. Invite students to compare this book to familiar folktales. Chart similarities and differences. Then, encourage the students to incorporate archetypal motifs and themes in stories of their own.

2. The author notes that the story was inspired by a sixteenth-century game that is still played today. Older children could research games of old, and, as an oral language activity, teach them to children in lower grades.

3. Heckedy Peg recites a chant in an attempt to gain entry into the children's home. The rhyme focuses on a description of the witch. Invite children to describe themselves in a chant that will be read by someone else in the class. Encourage the children to try to guess who wrote the chant by listening closely to the description.

4. Much of this story revolves around food and a mother's love for her children. In celebration of food and parenthood, plan and prepare a feast to be enjoyed by the children and their parents. Encourage the children to design and write invitations, compose and present tributes to their parents, and "act out" *Heckedy Peg* as Readers Theatre.

Related Books

Other folktales that feature trickery as a theme:

Aardema, Verna. *Rabbit Makes a Monkey of Lion: A Swahili Tale.*

Bang, Molly. *Wiley and the Hairy Man: Adapted from an American Folk Tale.*

Conover, Chris. *Mother Goose and the Sly Fox.*

Goble, Paul. *Iktomi and the Buffalo Skull: A Plains Indian Story.*

Goble, Paul. *Iktomi and the Ducks: A Plains Indian Story.*

Hyman, Trina Schart. *Little Red Riding Hood.*

Kesey, Ken. *Little Tricker the Squirrel Meets Big Double the Bear.*

Kimmel, Eric A. *Nanny Goat and the Seven Little Kids.*

McKissack, Patricia. *Flossie and the Fox.*

Snyder, Dianne. *The Boy of the Three-Year Nap.*

Young, Ed. *Lon Po Po: A Red-Riding Hood Story from China.*

Folklore titles in which one character outwits another:

Aardema, Verna. *Bimwili and the Zimwi: A Tale from Zanzibar.*

dePaola, Tomie. *Fin M'Coul: The Giant of Knockmany Hill.*

Morimoto, Junko. *The Inch Boy.*

Young, Ed. *The Terrible Nung Gwama: A Chinese Folktale.*

This book could also be compared to Anthony Browne's, Susan Jeffers's, and others' versions of *Hansel and Gretel.*

—by Cheryl Grossman

24 The High Rise Glorious Skittle Skat Roarious Sky Pie Angel Food Cake

Nancy Willard. *The High Rise Glorious Skittle Skat Roarious Sky Pie Angel Food Cake.* Illustrated by Richard Jesse Watson. San Diego: Harcourt Brace Jovanovich, 1990. ISBN 0-15-234332-6.

Plot Summary

When a young girl asks her mother what she wants for her birthday, the mother replies, "A birthday cake. You could make me a birthday cake." The mother then goes on to tell of the wonderful birthday cake her grandmother made for her when she was seven: a High Rise Glorious Skittle Skat Roarious Sky Pie Angel Food Cake. So, the daughter reads through thirty-two notebooks left to her by her great-grandmother, the cake baker. The notebooks contain poetry, newspaper clippings, and recipes—even a recipe for angel food cake—but not the recipe for this special cake. The recipe eventually turns up—in the piano—and the young girl discovers that the secret ingredient is to spread the sugar on a plate and write "EVOL" in the sugar with one's finger before adding it to the cake batter. Following other instructions from the recipe, the young girl sets her alarm and wakes up to bake the cake at midnight. Three angels appear, however, and eat the cake warm from the oven. But by morning another cake is baked, this one with a golden thimble just like the cake from long ago. From the wonderful title to the words on the final page, readers will be moved by Willard's beautiful choice of language and by the memorable images that she creates.

Teaching Suggestions

1. This is a wonderful book to read aloud in the classroom. Children love reciting the title, and they delight in the warm family story, which has just a hint of fantasy. Teachers generally find that the book evokes much conversation among children.

2. The great-grandmother's notebooks could be compared to journals or family scrapbooks. Children might consider the items that various family members keep. They could also be encouraged to keep notebooks of their own, in which they might record and collect thoughts, lists, drawings, clippings, poems—anything they may want to remember, hold on to, or simply jot down.

3. In addition to poems, news clippings, and recipes, the great-grandmother kept sayings in her notebook as well. One saying, "Grief in the evening is joy in the morning," connects with the story. Children might consider old sayings from folk wisdom and discuss how these sayings emerge and whether there is any truth in them.

4. This story revolves around a mother's memory from her own childhood. As such, the book has potential for eliciting family stories and memories and emphasizing their importance.

5. The "secret ingredient" is likely to be a point of discussion. One by one the children in one first-grade classroom figured out the meaning of writing "EVOL" in the sugar.

Related Books   Other books about family memories and traditions:

Ackerman, Karen. *Song and Dance Man.*

Duke, Kate. *Aunt Isabel Tells a Good One.*

Flournoy, Valerie. *The Patchwork Quilt.*

Geras, Adele. *My Grandmother's Stories: A Collection of Jewish Folk Tales.*

Howard, Elizabeth Fitzgerald. *Aunt Flossie's Hats (and Crab Cakes Later).*

Johnson, Angela. *Tell Me a Story, Mama.*

McDonald, Megan. *The Potato Man.*

Orr, Katherine Shelley. *My Grandpa and the Sea.*

Polacco, Patricia. *Thunder Cake.*

Rylant, Cynthia. *The Relatives Came.*

Students could also compare this book to Nancy Willard's *Pish, Posh, Said Hieronymus Bosch.*

—by Carol Avery

If You Were a Writer

Joan Lowery Nixon. *If You Were a Writer.* Illustrated by Bruce Degen. New York: Four Winds Press, 1988. ISBN 0-02-768210-2.

Suggested Grade Levels: 2–4

Plot Summary

Melia admires her mother, a writer, and wishes that she could write stories too. She watches her mother's fingers bounce over the typewriter and notices that sometimes she stares at the paper and sits as still as if she had been "turned to stone by an evil spell." Her mother explains that a writer does more than type; a writer works with words and tries to think of words that make pictures. Melia tries it and finds that her mother's silky blouse brings words like "slippery, slithery, and soft" to mind. Words become a game, a game that even Melia's younger sister sometimes plays. Mother also explains how a writer searches everywhere for ideas and describes how an author must ask "what if." Finally, Melia tries out what she has learned and begins to tell a story to her sister. Degen's bright, lively illustrations, done in pen-and-ink and watercolor, aptly capture this story.

Teaching Suggestions

1. The mother's helpful suggestions about writing, coupled with Melia's enthusiastic responses, could make this story a stepping stone for young writers. Children could discuss the writing process as Melia's mother sees it and compare this description to their own processes.

2. Children could list groups of words from the story that describe the senses. This activity could be extended by making charts that web each sense. Children could then add to their webs over a period of time. The webs might also be posted as a resource for the children's own writing.

3. Invite a local author to discuss his or her career with the class. This discussion could be extended by talking about our own careers and could even become a "mentoring experience."

4. View the films *Storymaker: Don Freeman* (Churchill Films), *The Story of a Book* (Pied Piper), and *Eric Carle: Imagemaker* (Philo-

mel). Each film tells the story of how a book got started, went through many drafts, and finally became a finished book.

Related Books   Other excellent books that explore the writing process:

Aliki. *How a Book Is Made.*

Asher, Sandy. *Where Do You Get Your Ideas? Helping Young Writers Begin.*

Broekel, Ray. *I Can Be an Author.*

Cassedy, Sylvia. *In Your Own Words: A Beginner's Guide to Writing.*

Dubrovin, Vivian. *Write Your Own Story.*

Goffstein, M. B. *A Writer.*

Hoban, Lillian. *Arthur's Pen Pal.*

Livingston, Myra Cohn. *Poem-making: Ways to Begin Writing Poetry.*

Snyder, Zilpha Keatley. *Libby on Wednesday.*

Tchudi, Susan J., and Stephen Tchudi. *The Young Writer's Handbook.*

Zinsser, William, and Jean Fritz. *Worlds of Childhood: The Art and Craft of Writing for Children.*

Books to help young writers get started:

Blume, Judy. *The Judy Blume Memory Book.*

Cleary, Beverly. *The Beezus and Ramona Diary.*

Cleary, Beverly. *The Ramona Quimby Diary.*

—by Carolyn J. Bauer

26 I'm in Charge of Celebrations

Byrd Baylor. *I'm in Charge of Celebrations.* Illustrated by Peter Parnall. New York: Charles Scribner's Sons, 1986. ISBN 0-684-18579-2.

Suggested Grade Levels: 3–8

Plot Summary

Most holidays and celebrations—religious holidays, national holidays, special commemorative days, weeks, or months—are planned according to an annual calendar of events. Others—birthday parties, school functions, picnics—are determined by the rituals within family and community groups. Yet we might also choose to celebrate the little day-to-day events in our lives. Poet Byrd Baylor does just that: "Last year I gave myself one hundred and eight celebrations—besides the ones that they close school for." Baylor's spontaneous celebrations of the desert are described in lyrical terms: "I wait until the white-winged doves are back from Mexico, and wildflowers cover the hills, and my favorite cactus blooms." And Parnall's fluid lines and warm desert tones beautifully reflect the quiet, poetic text.

Teaching Suggestions

1. Watch the videotape of Baylor reading this book: *Byrd Baylor: Storyteller* from the Southwest Series in Tucson, Arizona. Have different people read the book aloud, and discuss how a reader's interpretation of the text might affect his or her oral expression.

2. If students have already seen the illustrations, have them close their eyes for a second reading. Ask them to make "mind pictures" of the different celebrations. Discuss why this may be difficult (or easy) to do after having seen the artist's work.

3. Students could explore how mood is expressed through words and illustrations. Encourage students to convey a mood through various mediums (e.g., dance, painting, writing).

4. Ask students what celebrations they would note as important in their own lives. Have them tell about these celebrations in a way that suits the particular celebration (e.g., the daily ritual of an early morning walk might be expressed through a dance performed for classmates). Students could also write poems that celebrate something special to them.

5. As a response to *I'm in Charge of Celebrations,* have students tear lightweight construction paper into images that represent a celebration that is important to them. Mount these images as a mosaic on a wall for a breathtaking display.

6. Students could discuss Baylor's interesting use of language and speculate on any poet's choices of "just the right words" to create evocative images.

Related Books

Similar books by Byrd Baylor:

The Desert Is Theirs
Desert Voices
Everybody Needs a Rock
The Way to Start a Day

Between Cattails by Terry Tempest Williams also celebrates nature.

Also see the videotape *Byrd Baylor: Storyteller,* from Southwest Series, Inc., in Tuscon, Arizona, and Paul B. Janeczko's *The Place My Words Are Looking For: What Poets Say About and Through Their Work.*

—by Marilou R. Sorensen

27 In the Year of the Boar and Jackie Robinson

Bette Bao Lord. *In the Year of the Boar and Jackie Robinson.* Illustrated by Marc Simont. New York: Harper and Row, 1984. ISBN 0-06-024003-2.

Suggested Grade Levels: 4–7

Plot Summary

A story cycle begins in January, the Chinese New Year, and travels through December's Star-Spangled Christmas. This particular cycle carries Bandit from the House of Wong, her ancestral home in China, to her new home in Brooklyn, where she becomes Shirley Temple Wong. The name change suggests the main character's striking transition from one culture to another. Shirley is a warm-hearted girl who learns how to play baseball and the piano and how to adjust to the group of older children who become her classmates. The insight gained from watching Shirley take on a second language and culture while not losing her Chinese heritage is this book's strong contribution to children's literature. The heroine's varied experiences while learning English provide a remarkable context for enjoyable reading that can lead to cultural understanding.

Teaching Suggestions

1. Students might interview older people who immigrated to America and find out what cultural stories, holidays, and foods they still share within their families.

2. Students could discuss the literary aspects of re-creating our past. Perhaps they could do a biographical study of Bette Bao Lord and determine how her own experiences might have led her to write this book.

3. Students could try writing an autobiographical account about an event in which their attitude was changed by someone else. Such an account could be elaborated on by fictionalizing parts of it.

4. Lord's book could be compared to those in the following bibliography. Students could study the authors of these books in order to determine how authors from diverse cultures effectively use their cultural experiences in the stories they write.

Related Books

The following books are written by authors whose own cultural experiences are reflected in their writing:

Buss, Fran Leeper. *Journey of the Sparrows.*

Chin, Frank. *Donald Duk.*

Choi, Sook Nyul. *Year of Impossible Goodbyes.*

Fox, Mem. *Koala Lou.*

Fox, Mem. *Possum Magic.*

Gilson, Jamie. *Hello, My Name Is Scrambled Eggs.*

Prochazkova, Iva. *The Season of Secret Wishes.*

Singer, Isaac Bashevis. *When Shlemiel Went to Warsaw and Other Stories.*

Taylor, Mildred D. *Roll of Thunder, Hear My Cry.*

Watkins, Yoko Kawashima. *So Far from the Bamboo Grove.*

Yep, Laurence. *Child of the Owl.*

Yep, Laurence. *The Rainbow People.*

Yep, Laurence. *The Star Fisher.*

—by Richard Van Dongen and Jill P. May

The Island

Gary Paulsen. *The Island*. New York: Orchard Books, 1988.
ISBN 0-531-05749-6.

Suggested Grade Levels: 6–9

Plot Summary

After his family moves from Madison to a cabin in the woods of northern Wisconsin, Wil Neuton must learn to adapt to an unfamiliar environment. Discouraged and lonely, he finds a small island on a nearby lake where he observes nature and writes in his diary. Through these activities, Wil learns valuable lessons about his past and about how he can enjoy his new life. And in learning about himself, Wil helps other people understand that being different is not necessarily a bad thing.

Teaching Suggestions

1. In reading through this novel, students could note the various stages of Wil's character development, listing two or three adjectives that best describe how the teenager feels as a result of the events or thoughts of each chapter.

2. Although Wil is alone during most of the novel, he does learn many things from the people he encounters. Have students make a list of each person he meets and discuss how these people contribute to his character growth.

3. Using Wil's writing as a model, students could keep their own journals in which they examine the importance of apparently simple things to them.

4. Have the students write a character study of an older person who is important to them.

Related Books

Other books that feature characters who keep diaries or journals:

Avi. *The True Confessions of Charlotte Doyle.*
Byars, Betsy. *The Burning Questions of Bingo Brown.*
Cameron, Eleanor. *The Private Worlds of Julia Redfern.*
Fitzhugh, Louise. *Harriet the Spy.*

Gleeson, Libby. *Eleanor, Elizabeth.*

Heinrich, Bernard. *An Owl in the House: A Naturalist's Diary.*

Holland, Isabelle. *Abbie's God Book.*

Klein, Robin. *Penny Pollard's Diary.*

Little, Jean. *Hey World, Here I Am!*

MacLachlan, Patricia. *Arthur, For the Very First Time.*

MacLachlan, Patricia. *Cassie Binegar.*

Marsden, John. *So Much to Tell You.*

O'Dell, Scott. *Island of the Blue Dolphins.*

Paulsen, Gary. *Hatchet.*

Roop, Peter, and Connie Roop. *I, Columbus: My Journal, 1492–1493.*

Selden, Bernice. *The Mill Girls: Lucy Larcom, Harriet Hanson Robinson, Sarah G. Bagley.*

Sharmat, Marjorie. *Chasing after Annie.*

Stevens, Carla. *A Book of Your Own: Keeping a Diary or Journal.*

Tolles, Martha. *Who's Reading Darci's Diary?*

Turner, Ann. *Nettie's Trip South.*

Van Leeuwen, Jean. *Dear Mom, You're Ruining My Life.*

Also see the list of related books for Avi's *The True Confessions of Charlotte Doyle.*

—by Jon C. Stott

29 The Jolly Postman; or, Other People's Letters

Janet Ahlberg and Allan Ahlberg. *The Jolly Postman; or, Other People's Letters.* Boston: Little, Brown, 1986. ISBN 0-316-02036-2.

Plot Summary

This delightful and innovative book is perfect for any child acquiring letter-writing skills. Told in rhyming verse, the story describes a postman who makes his rounds delivering letters to such folktale notables as the Three Bears, the Wicked Witch, Jack's Giant, the Big Bad Wolf, Cinderella, and Goldilocks. Many forms of letter writing are included in the book. The Three Bears, for instance, receive an apology note from Goldilocks. The Wicked Witch is sent a catalogue of items that the typical witch might need. Jack sends a picture postcard to the giant informing him of the ideal vacation he is having. Attorneys employed by Red Riding Hood and the Three Pigs send a letter of warning to the wolf. And Goldilocks receives a birthday card from Mrs. Bunting and her baby of nursery rhyme fame. Children will enjoy this glimpse into the mailboxes of characters from their favorite fairy tales.

Teaching Suggestions

1. While the class views the postcard Jack sends to the giant, conduct a discussion that focuses on what makes a postcard interesting and enjoyable to read. For further analysis, read the postcards in *Stringbean's Trip to the Shining Sea* by Vera Williams. Invite students to design picture postcards of their own city or of countries they are studying. Send these to prearranged pen pals to begin a letter-writing exchange.

2. Plan a storybook character birthday party. Encourage each child to dress as a favorite character from folk literature. As part of the day's festivities, have the children create an appropriate birthday card to send from their character to another character attending the party.

3. Compare the language and form used in the friendly letters included in the book to the more formal conventions of business letters. Throughout the year, encourage students to use their letter-writing knowledge and skills for authentic purposes. Possibilities might include sending for field trip information, composing thank-you letters to volunteer parents, exchanging ongoing communication between teachers and children, establishing pen pal ties between the children and published authors or local scientists, inviting others to class events, or mailing letters to the editor about "burning" issues.

4. In one illustration, the postman is reading a newspaper in the witch's house. Create a newspaper in the classroom that includes current news stories on the lives of storybook characters.

5. Following the format of *The Jolly Postman; or, Other People's Letters,* plan a Jolly Postman Big Book. Brainstorm other fairy tale characters that the postman could visit and invite the children to write letters that will slip in and out of envelopes. New letters could be written periodically to replace the old.

Related Books   The following are other books that use letter writing as a focus:

Ahlberg, Janet, and Allan Ahlberg. *The Jolly Christmas Postman.*

Alexander, Sue. *Dear Phoebe.*

Asch, Frank, and Vladimir Vagin. *Dear Brother.*

Baker, Keith. *The Dove's Letter.*

Brandt, Betty. *Special Delivery.*

Brisson, Pat. *Your Best Friend, Kate.*

Brisson, Pat. *Kate Heads West.*

Brisson, Pat. *Kate on the Coast.*

Caseley, Judith. *Dear Annie.*

Dragonwagon, Crescent. *Dear Miss Moshki.*

Gibbons, Gail. *The Post Office Book: Mail and How It Moves.*

Haley, Gail. *Post Office Cat.*

James, Simon. *Dear Mr. Blueberry.*

Joslin, Sesyle. *Dear Dragon . . .*

Leedy, Loreen. *Messages in the Mailbox: How to Write a Letter.*

Legum, Margaret. *Mailbox, Quailbox.*

Marshak, Samuil. *Hail to Mail.*

Mischel, Florence. *How to Write a Letter.*

Parker, Nancy Winslow. *Love from Aunt Betty.*
Rylant, Cynthia. *Mr. Griggs' Work.*
Shulevitz, Uri. *Toddlecreek Post Office.*
Williams, Vera. *Stringbean's Trip to the Shining Sea.*
Zimelman, Nathan. *Please Excuse Jasper.*

—by Cheryl Grossman

Joyful Noise: Poems for Two Voices

Paul Fleischman. *Joyful Noise: Poems for Two Voices.* Illustrated by Eric Beddows. New York: Harper and Row, 1988. ISBN 0-06-021852-5.

Suggested Grade Levels: 4–8

Plot Summary

This remarkably imaginative volume of poetry captures the "joyful noise" of insects. Each poem, designed so that the lines can be read by two voices either alternatively or in harmony, hums with the buzzing, droning, and swarming of the various insects described. Because of the sophisticated references and free verse form, most of the pieces will be more appealing to older children. A poem like "House Crickets," however, with its repetitive refrain of "cricket," or "Whirligig Beetles," with its rhythmic description of movement, will attract younger listeners. The imaginative and unique images used to describe each insect are complemented by black-and-white illustrations that show each insect in detail as it creeps, crawls, or flies across the page. This book is a well-deserved winner of the Newbery Medal.

Teaching Suggestions

1. A natural activity to do with this book is choral reading. As partners, children could create a choral reading or Readers Theatre presentation. The same could be done for Fleischman's *I Am Phoenix*, a collection of bird poems. Then comparisons could be made.

2. Teachers could encourage children to examine the words Fleischman chooses to describe each insect. The class might discuss why these choices are effective in conveying each insect's "personality."

3. Children could compare individual poems in the book to those on the same topic in Mary Ann Hoberman's *Bugs*, noting the different words and images that each poet uses to describe the same insects.

4. Children could also consider how Fleischman has created rhythm through different rhyme schemes, alternating lines, and similar techniques.

5. Children could be asked to write their own insect poems and accompanying scientific descriptions.

Related Books

Other collections of poetry about insects:

Hoberman, Mary Ann. *Bugs.*

Hopkins, Lee Bennett. *Flit, Flutter, Fly! Poems about Bugs and Other Crawly Creatures.*

Norman, Charles. *The Hornbeam Tree and Other Poems.*

Singer, Marilyn. *Turtle in July.*

Books about insects, bugs, and other ''creepy crawlies'':

Carle, Eric. *The Very Quiet Cricket.*

Norsgaard, E. Jaediker. *How to Raise Butterflies.*

O'Toole, Christopher. *Discovering Flies.*

Parker, Nancy Winslow, and Joan Richards Wright. *Bugs.*

Parsons, Alexandra. *Amazing Spiders.*

Patent, Dorothy Hinshaw. *The Lives of Spiders.*

See Fleischman's *I Am Phoenix: Poems for Two Voices* for a similar book of poetry about birds.

—by Amy McClure

Knots on a Counting Rope

Bill Martin, Jr., and John Archambault. *Knots on a Counting Rope.* Illustrated by Ted Rand. New York: Henry Holt, 1987. ISBN 0-8050-0571-4.

Suggested Grade Levels: 1–3

Plot Summary

All children love to hear stories about themselves, and the Native American child in this story is no different. He sits in rapt attention as his grandfather relates the story of his difficult birth, and how, in spite of his blindness, he has grown in strength and courage until he now deserves his given name, "Boy-Strength-of-Blue-Horses." As the story is told, just as every time it has been told in the past, the grandfather ties another knot in the counting rope, symbolizing the passage of time and reminding the boy that his grandfather will not always be with him. In a poignant exchange between the boy and his grandfather, the child is reassured that when his grandfather dies, the boy will be "strong enough to cross the dark mountains" and that the grandfather's love will always be there "with the strength of blue horses."

Told in poetic prose, the mounting tension of the boy's quest to overcome darkness in a bareback riding race is supported by short, staccato sentences and descriptive text. Peaceful scenes with the boy and his grandfather are written almost lyrically. For example, in describing the wind to his grandfather, the boy says, "The wind is my friend, Grandfather. / It throws back my hair and laughs on my face." Color is also used effectively to convey mood. The vibrant yellow light at the boy's naming ceremony contrasts sharply with the dark sky as Grandfather races through a wind storm to bring Grandmother to witness her grandchild's birth. With the text's emphasis on rhythm and sensory images of sound and touch, this book begs to be read aloud.

Teaching Suggestions

1. The young boy elicits his story from the grandfather through a set of carefully worded questions. Children could plan to ask close family members similar questions in order to learn their own life stories. The stories could be audiotaped and played as part of a "child-of-the-week" program.

2. Children could participate in an oral history interview with an older member of their family to determine the significant events and experiences in that individual's childhood. Photographs and other memorabilia could be gathered and displayed with the written histories.

3. When the boy in the story is born, his grandfather takes him to "see the morning" just at the moment two great blue horses come galloping by. The boy raises his arms to the horses and is thus named "Boy-Strength-of-Blue-Horses." Discuss the symbolism of Native American names with children. Ask them to consider a suitable name for themselves and to use felt on burlap or other materials to illustrate a scene that symbolically conveys their name. These scenes could be displayed with a written explanation of how the name is a metaphor for a part of their personality.

4. Since the young boy in the story is blind, his grandfather encourages the boy to experience the world through his other senses. The boy hears the sunrise through the song of the birds, describes the sky as "soft, like lambs' wool," and feels blue as happiness in his heart. Older children might enjoy the opportunity to describe the things they see through their other senses. Post these descriptions throughout the room and encourage the children to use the descriptions in their writing when appropriate.

Related Books

The following books also feature an older family member relating stories to the younger generation:

Ackerman, Karen. *Song and Dance Man.*

Cech, John. *My Grandmother's Journey.*

Clifford, Eth. *The Remembering Box.*

Dorros, Arthur. *Abuela.*

Duke, Kate. *Aunt Isabel Tells a Good One.*

Flournoy, Valerie. *The Patchwork Quilt.*

Geras, Adele. *My Grandmother's Stories: A Collection of Jewish Folk Tales.*

Hoffman, Mary. *Amazing Grace.*

Howard, Elizabeth Fitzgerald. *Aunt Flossie's Hat (and Crab Cakes Later).*

Johnston, Angela. *Tell Me a Story, Mama.*

MacLachlan, Patricia. *Through Grandpa's Eyes.*

Miles, Miska. *Annie and the Old One.*

Polacco, Patricia. *Thunder Cake.*

Stolz, Mary. *Go Fish.*

Velarde, Pablita. *Old Father Story Teller.*

Wallace-Brodeur, Ruth. *Stories from the Big Chair.*

—by Cheryl Grossman

32 Little Tricker the Squirrel Meets Big Double the Bear

Ken Kesey. *Little Tricker the Squirrel Meets Big Double the Bear.* Illustrated by Barry Moser. New York: Viking, 1990. ISBN 0-670-81136-X.

Suggested Grade Levels: All ages

Plot Summary

Tricker the Squirrel lies awake in his bed thinking about the hazelnuts, which are almost ready to be harvested. Suddenly, the morning quiet is broken by the arrival of a huge high-country bear to Topple's Bottom: "A-ROARRR! . . . I'm Big Double from the high wild ridges, and I'm double big and I'm double bad and I'm double hungry a-roarrr!" One by one, the bear encounters Charlie Charles the Woodchuck, Longrellers the Rabbit, and Sally Snipsister the Marten and devours them. Then he meets Little Tricker the Squirrel. Through a hilarious sequence of events, Tricker outwits the bear and frees the swallowed characters.

Ken Kesey, author of *One Flew Over the Cuckoo's Nest* and *Sometimes a Great Notion,* here writes a tale first told to him by his Grandma Smith. He captures the storyteller's voice in all its rhythm and Appalachian color.

Teaching Suggestions

1. This is an excellent book to read aloud, though a reader might want to practice before presenting it to a group. The group could then discuss some of the words, phrases, and idioms that reflect the story's cultural origins and delight the ear.

2. Kesey uses various spellings, sentence structures, even style and size of print to re-create the voice of the storyteller. Explore these graphics with students and discuss how form can serve a writer's purpose. Students could be encouraged to experiment with different graphics in their own writing.

3. This book lends itself to a discussion about storytelling as an art. Students might collect stories from senior citizens in their own families as Kesey has done. Some students might choose to write or orally retell these stories.

4. The role of the storyteller in particular cultures could be examined using examples of stories told in various parts of the country. Kesey's story could be compared to other Appalachian folktales.

5. Students could create a story map of Big Double's encounters with the various characters. Then they could compare this pattern of encounters to patterns of events in other folktales.

Related Books

Other examples of Appalachian folklore:

Chase, Richard. *Grandfather Tales: American-English Folk Tales.*

Chase, Richard. *The Jack Tales.*

Galdone, Joanna. *The Tailypo: A Ghost Story.*

Haley, Gail E. *Jack and the Bean Tree.*

Hooks, William H. *The Three Little Pigs and the Fox.*

Lester, Julius. *The Tales of Uncle Remus: The Adventures of Brer Rabbit.*

Lester, Julius. *More Tales of Uncle Remus: Further Adventures of Brer Rabbit, His Friends, Enemies, and Others.*

Lewis, J. Patrick. *The Moonbow of Mr. B. Bones.*

McKissack, Patricia. *Flossie and the Fox.*

Parks, Van Dyke, and Malcolm Jones. *Jump! The Adventures of Brer Rabbit.*

Parks, Van Dyke, and Malcolm Jones. *Jump Again! More Adventures of Brer Rabbit.*

Still, James, and Margot Tomes. *Jack and the Wonder Beans.*

Van Laan, Nancy. *Possum Come A-Knockin'.*

See the list of related books for Audrey Wood's *Heckedy Peg* for examples of trickster stories.

—by Carol Avery

Lyddie

Katherine Paterson. *Lyddie*. New York: E. P. Dutton, 1991.
ISBN 0-525-67338-5.

Suggested Grade Levels: 4–8

Plot Summary

Tough, resilient, and responsible, thirteen-year-old Lyddie feels driven to take care of everything and everyone. With their father gone long ago to find work elsewhere and their mother and sisters off to live with an uncle, Lyddie and ten-year-old Charles tend the farm alone. Then word comes that their mother has "let" the farm to a neighbor and hired the children out to work. Finally driven almost to despair about the family debt, Lyddie makes her way to the mills in Lowell, Massachusetts. Here she can work for a wage, save her money to redeem the farm, and reunite her family. Life seldom follows a plan, however, and Lyddie must soon make new decisions and living arrangements. Her mother and one sister die, Charles and another sister are willingly and lovingly adopted, and the farm is sold. Dismissed at the mill for "moral turpitude," Lyddie journeys home to say goodbye to the farm. It is there that she makes the decision to use what money she has earned to take herself to Oberlin College in Ohio.

Lyddie is a well-told story of a strong, determined girl who grows into an even stronger and more self-reliant woman. Lyddie confronts life with energy and ability. Not only does she acquire valuable work skills, but she also comes to understand herself and others with depth and insight. She recognizes the love and goodness of her Quaker neighbors, the injustice of slavery, and the need to fight for better working conditions and health care in the mills. Both *Lyddie* the book and Lyddie the character represent a slice of American social change and history.

Teaching Suggestions

1. Class members could keep individual or whole-class journals of Lyddie's experiences.

2. Because the story covers a time of much social change, it lends itself to research, discussion, and reporting in areas such as slavery and the underground railroad, the role of women and

children in the early factories, the role of Quakers in New England history, working and living conditions in the mill towns, and the educational opportunities available at the time.

3. The class could create comparison charts depicting life in the mill towns and on the farms in 1843 and now.

4. The vocabulary used in 1843 was considerably different from that used today. This book provides the opportunity to explore these differences. Examples might include "let the farm," "hired out," "lock out," or "moral turpitude."

5. Lyddie, Luke, Diana, Charles, and Rachel are distinctive enough people around whom to create character descriptions in the form of a graffiti board or character map.

6. Dickens's *Oliver Twist* would be an ideal book to read aloud to the class, since this is one of the books Lyddie purchases with her hard-earned money. Students could compare the working conditions described in Dickens's book to those depicted in Paterson's *Lyddie*.

Related Books   Other books featuring characters and working life in earlier times:

Beatty, Patricia. *Jayhawker.*

Beatty, Patricia. *Sarah and Me and the Lady from the Sea.*

Collier, James Lincoln, and Christopher Collier. *The Clock.*

Doherty, Berlie. *Granny Was a Buffer Girl.*

Macaulay, David. *Mill.*

Selden, Bernice. *The Mill Girls: Lucy Larcom, Harriet Hanson Robinson, Sarah G. Bagley.*

Smucker, Barbara. *Runaway to Freedom: A Story of the Underground Railway.*

Talbot, Charlene Joy. *An Orphan for Nebraska.*

—by Rachael Hungerford

34 The Magical Adventures of Pretty Pearl

Virginia Hamilton. *The Magical Adventures of Pretty Pearl.* New York: Harper and Row, 1983. ISBN 0-06-022186-0.

Suggested Grade Levels: 5–8

Plot Summary

Pretty Pearl is a god child living on beautiful Mount Highness in Kenya. She feels she is getting into "god power" too fast and seeks permission from her older brother, the most powerful of the gods, John de Conquer, to step down from the mountain in order to be among humankind. Disguised as albatrosses, the two sail above a slave ship to the Georgia colony, where the sorrows of the black people move Pretty Pearl to act on their behalf. John gives her a magical necklace to help in times of need and some advice about using her powers. Hamilton uses folklore, legend, and history to weave a cultural tapestry rich in metaphor, speech patterns, and dialects, with an overarching theme of the caring bond within and among ethnic groups.

Teaching Suggestions

1. This book affords an excellent opportunity for children to learn more about the folk character John de Conquer. Students can deduce a description of his appearance, his character, and his powers from the story. Then they could read Zora Neale Hurston's description of his origins in Langston Hughes and Arna Bontemps's *The Book of Negro Folklore* and discuss likenesses and differences.

2. The folk character John Henry Roustabout appears as another older brother of Pretty Pearl. Children could read other John Henry books and compare his role as an American folk character to the presentation of him in this book.

3. Have children note examples of speech patterns and dialects from different parts of the book. They could read Priscilla Jaquith's *Bo Rabbit Smart for True* and Lorenz Graham's *David He No Fear* to become familiar with some of these speech patterns.

4. Children could explore the relationship between African Americans and Native Americans. What can they learn about the culture of the two peoples?

5. Compare the writing style in this book to that of other books by Virginia Hamilton, such as *Arilla Sun Down*.

Related Books

Other books of African American folklore:

Bang, Molly. *Wiley and the Hairy Man: Adapted from an American Folk Tale.*

Brooke, William J. *A Telling of the Tales: Five Stories.*

Bryan, Ashley. *Turtle Knows Your Name.*

Felton, Harold. *John Henry and His Hammer.*

Graham, Lorenz. *David He No Fear.*

Harris, Joel. *Jump! The Adventures of Brer Rabbit.*

Harris, Joel. *Jump Again! More Adventures of Brer Rabbit.*

Hughes, Langston, and Arna Bontemps. *The Book of Negro Folklore.*

Jaquith, Priscilla. *Bo Rabbit Smart for True: Folktales from the Gullah.*

Keats, Ezra Jack. *John Henry, An American Legend.*

Killens, John. *A Man Ain't Nothin' But a Man: The Adventures of John Henry.*

McKissack, Patricia. *A Million Fish—More or Less.*

Sanfield, Steve. *The Adventures of High John the Conqueror.*

This book could be compared to others by Hamilton, including *Arilla Sun Down, In the Beginning: Creation Myths from Around the World,* and *The People Could Fly: American Black Folktales.*

—by Inga Kromann-Kelly

The Mysteries of Harris Burdick

Chris Van Allsburg. *The Mysteries of Harris Burdick.* Boston: Houghton Mifflin, 1984. ISBN 0-395-35393-9.

Suggested Grade Levels: 3 and up

Plot Summary

Years ago, a man by the name of Harris Burdick allegedly left a publisher drawings, captions, and titles for each of fourteen stories, but he never returned. Chris Van Allsburg has combined these titles with compelling black-and-white illustrations to convey mysterious images such as a vine growing out of an open book, a house lifting off of its foundation like a spaceship, and tiny lights entering a dark room through an open window. No narrative thread connects the drawings, which are linked only by the idea of the unexplained or supernatural. Each picture and title provokes the reader to consider the possibilities for the story that might follow. One is left wondering what the original author had in mind and what other interpretations—other than Van Allsburg's—might have followed from such titles. The illustrations stimulate the imagination, compelling children to create their own stories in response to the pictures.

Teaching Suggestions

1. Van Allsburg's book leads the reader to observe from unusual vantage points. Ask students to determine where the audience is in each of the illustrations. For example, in "Uninvited Guests," the reader is under the stairs. Discuss how these vantage points add to the interest of the "story."

2. Use each picture as a story starter for either oral or written work. The word "Mysteries" in the title suggests that there might be clues, background material, or various solutions that could be developed. Encourage students to look for such information, to embellish on Van Allsburg's work, and to incorporate such components of mystery in their own writing.

3. Using the evidence he provides in his illustrations, discuss how Van Allsburg seems to have interpreted each of the titles. Have students illustrate or write about alternative interpretations.

4. The illustrations are done in pencil on Strathmore paper. Have students try a small drawing using these materials to find out why they are effective. Introduce terms such as *value* (e.g., light and dark), *intensity* (e.g., bright and dull), and *use of line* (e.g., width, length, direction, focus, and boundary). Discuss how Van Allsburg has used these qualities to his advantage.

5. The illustrations have formal properties such as theme, symmetry, rhythm, repetition, and dominance. Have students find examples of these properties and compare them to examples found in other works by Van Allsburg.

Related Books

Books that provoke readers to react to clues in the text:

Base, Graeme. *The Eleventh Hour: A Curious Mystery.*
Shannon, George. *Stories to Solve: Folktales from Around the World.*
Williams, Kit. *Masquerade.*

Other books by Van Allsburg that could be compared to this one:

Ben's Dream
The Garden of Abdul Gasazi
Jumanji
The Polar Express
The Sweetest Fig
The Widow's Broom
The Wreck of the Zephyr
The Wretched Stone

—by Marilou R. Sorensen

Nettie's Trip South

Ann Turner. *Nettie's Trip South*. Illustrated by Ronald Himler.
New York: Macmillan, 1987. ISBN 0-02-789240-9.

Suggested Grade Levels: 4–6

Plot Summary

In a story inspired by her great-grandmother's diary, which chronicled her travels from Albany, New York, to Richmond, Virginia, as a young girl in 1859, Turner reveals Nettie's heart-wrenching observations of slavery prior to the Civil War. In a letter she writes to her best friend, Nettie sadly recalls Tabith, a black maid at a Richmond hotel who has no last name. She remembers the buggy ride to a plantation where a grandfather is lying on a makeshift bed of rags. "Animals live better," writes Nettie. At a slave auction—her most searing memory—she witnesses two eight-year-old children holding hands who are forced apart and sold separately.

Turner has done a masterful job of reporting history from a child's point of view. Nettie's innocent thoughts are effectively captured in passages such as "Addie, I was so worried I was almost sick. Julie told me slaves are thought to be three-fifths of a person. It's in the constitution. I'd never seen a slave and wondered, what were they missing?" Her poignant reactions to the slave auction are interwoven with a historically accurate description of the inhuman treatment of blacks during this turbulent period in history.

This book is an exemplary model of historical fiction. It pays strict attention to historical detail while at the same time demonstrates how past events affected people's lives. Nettie's observation that "If we slipped into a black skin like a tight coat, everything would change" has as much meaning for her as it does for us today.

Teaching Suggestions

1. Nettie is given the opportunity to travel south with her brother Lockwood, a newspaper reporter who is on his first assignment. Discuss Nettie's reaction to what she sees. Then discuss what her brother might have reported. Invite students to imagine they are Lockwood and ask them to write a newspaper article reporting their observations. Students could select from a variety of subjects: work on the plantation, living conditions, the slave

auction, differences between life in Albany and life in Richmond, and so on.

2. Letter-writing opportunities abound as a response to this book. The children could imagine themselves as abolitionists writing letters of protest to newspapers. They could put themselves in the shoes of the children who are separated at the auction block and write letters revealing their inner thoughts. Or they could opt to be Addie writing a letter in response to Nettie's correspondence. Finally, children could be asked to consider human rights injustices in today's world and write persuasive letters expressing their concerns to appropriate members of the political administration.

3. The issue of slavery was the newsmaking issue of Nettie's day. Encourage students to keep a journal, not only to record daily occurrences in their own lives, but also to reflect on their views regarding the current events reported in the newspaper and on television news. These reflections could be shared periodically and would be likely to spark lively classroom discussion.

Related Books

Other picture books that feature accounts of historical events from a child's perspective:

Ackerman, Karen. *The Tin Heart.*

Armstrong, Jennifer. *Steal Away.*

Collier, James Lincoln, and Christopher Collier. *Jump Ship to Freedom.*

Fleischman, Paul. *Bull Run.*

Fritz, Jean. *Brady.*

Hansen, Joyce. *Out from this Place.*

Harvey, Brett. *My Prairie Year: Based on the Diary of Elenore Plaisted.*

Kinsey-Warnock, Natalie. *Wilderness Cat.*

Leighton, Maxinne. *An Ellis Island Christmas.*

Lester, Julius. *To Be a Slave.*

Lyon, George Ella. *Cecil's Story.*

Marie, D. *Tears for Ashan.*

Meadowcroft, Enid La Monte. *Silver for General Washington.*

Moore, Yvette. *Freedom Songs.*

Turner, Ann. *Katie's Trunk.*

Winter, Jeanette. *Follow the Drinking Gourd.*

—by Cheryl Grossman

The News about Dinosaurs

37

Patricia Lauber. *The News about Dinosaurs.* New York: Bradbury Press, 1989. ISBN 0-02-754520-2.

Suggested Grade Levels: 3–8

Plot Summary

This well-organized and vividly illustrated book presents factual, up-to-the-minute information about dinosaurs. Lauber systematically introduces the study of dinosaurs, a wide variety of dinosaur species, and information about their appearance, habits, and habitats. The special format of the book juxtaposes prior knowledge of dinosaurs, which was based on incomplete information, against "The News Is . . . ," as determined by current researchers. Full-color illustrations from several different sources follow the text closely in presenting an accurate vision of what we currently know to be true. A pronunciation guide, which offers fascinating examples of the latest dinosaur names, and an index extend the usefulness of the book as a reference tool.

An honor book for the first NCTE Orbis Pictus award for outstanding nonfiction for children, *The News about Dinosaurs* is an excellent example of how the best nonfiction can hold its own as interesting and high-quality literature. Lauber's book reveals that "facts" change as we gather more information about our world, showing clearly where mistaken assumptions occurred in the past and what kind of information was needed to set the record straight (e.g., fossilized bones, eggs, footprints). What's more, Lauber walks the reader through the processes of scientific inquiry and deductive thinking in several specific examples. Yet the tone is never tedious. Even children who are not especially "dinosaur-crazy" will respond to the style of writing. Fascinating facts are shared in powerful prose.

Teaching Suggestions

1. Reading or browsing through this book should lead to a lively discussion. Questions such as the following might be considered: What other things are changing in science (e.g., space

exploration, evolution, computer technology)? How might future information challenge what we currently know or believe?

2. Such a book also suggests comparison activities. Students could list the differences now known to exist between dinosaurs and reptiles or contrast old dinosaur information with the new discoveries. The book could also be compared to a previous book by Lauber, *Dinosaurs Walked Here and Other Stories Fossils Tell,* or to dinosaur books by other authors (see *New Questions and Answers about Dinosaurs* by Seymour Simon and *Dinosaur Dig* by Kathryn Lasky).

3. Students might also enjoy writing their own "The News Is . . ." reports about subjects that particularly interest them. Gathering information might include conducting interviews, reading newspapers, and writing letters in order to contrast old and new knowledge. Encourage students to try developing glossaries and indexes as Lauber has done.

4. If the opportunity is available and the response to the book is strong, students might enjoy a visit to a natural history museum for a close examination of fossils or skeletons.

Related Books

Other useful books about dinosaurs:

Aliki. *Digging Up Dinosaurs.*
Aliki. *Dinosaur Bones.*
Aliki. *Dinosaurs Are Different.*
Aliki. *Fossils Tell of Long Ago.*
Arnold, Caroline. *Dinosaur Mountain: Graveyard of the Past.*
Barton, Byron. *Bones, Bones, Dinosaur Bones.*
Cobb, Vicki. *The Monsters Who Died: A Mystery about Dinosaurs.*
Craig, M. Jean. *Dinosaurs and More Dinosaurs.*
Freedman, Russell. *Dinosaurs and Their Young.*
Hopkins, Lee Bennett. *Dinosaurs.*
Lasky, Kathryn. *The Bone Wars.*
Lasky, Kathryn. *Dinosaur Dig.*
Lauber, Patricia. *Dinosaurs Walked Here and Other Stories Fossils Tell.*
Milton, Joyce. *Dinosaur Days.*
Prelutsky, Jack. *Tyrannosaurus Was a Beast.*
Sattler, Helen Roney. *Baby Dinosaurs.*
Sattler, Helen Roney. *The New Illustrated Dinosaur Dictionary.*

Simon, Seymour. *New Questions and Answers about Dinosaurs.*

Simon, Seymour. *The Smallest Dinosaurs.*

Taylor, Paul D. *Fossil.*

Thomson, Peggy. *Auks, Rocks, and the Odd Dinosaur: Inside Stories from the Smithsonian's Museum of Natural History.*

Walton, Rick, and Ann Walton. *Fossil Follies! Jokes about Dinosaurs.*

Yolen, Jane. *Dinosaur Dances.*

—by Sylvia M. Vardell

One-Eyed Cat

Paula Fox. *One-Eyed Cat.* Scarsdale, NY: Bradbury Press, 1984.
ISBN 0-02-735540-3.

Suggested Grade Levels: 5–8

Plot Summary

Eleven-year-old Nat is almost sure that the wild one-eyed cat living in the woods is the one he accidentally wounded with a gun his father had forbidden him to use. The cat in this novel thus becomes a symbol of Nat's struggle to deal with a growing burden of guilt. At the same time, Nat must also come to terms with his mother's invalidism, his father's smoldering "goodness," his Uncle Hilary's generosity, and his own preoccupation with the elderly Mr. Scully. Although the book is psychologically and morally complex, the simple prose draws readers in to experience new understandings about such issues as the human experience of guilt, the pain of separation, and the struggle to be a "good" person. This book won a 1985 Newbery honor award.

Teaching Suggestions

1. This is a good book to use to explore how foreshadowing helps the reader predict what might happen next. Students could keep an ongoing chart of how the author uses this technique.

2. Students could explore how the characters are changed by the events that happen in the novel. One way to do this is through the use of character sociograms.

3. Authors sometimes use the metaphor of the seasons to set a mood in their stories. Invite students to explore this writing technique by finding examples in the story.

4. Ask students to determine whose point of view the author is reflecting in the plot. They might consider how third-person narrative affects one's interpretation of events in a novel.

5. Students could discuss how and why the cat is a symbol in this story. This discussion could lead to an investigation of the use of symbols in other books. Encourage students to consider different objects or animals and what they might represent.

Related Books

The following books also have characters who deal with guilt and hidden feelings:

Bauer, Marion Dane. *On My Honor.*

Bawden, Nina. *Carrie's War.*

Fox, Paula. *The Stone-Faced Boy.*

MacLachlan, Patricia. *Cassie Binegar.*

Paterson, Katherine. *Bridge to Terabithia.*

Paulsen, Gary. *Popcorn Days and Buttermilk Nights.*

Smith, Doris Buchanan. *A Taste of Blackberries.*

—by Jill P. May and Inga Kromann-Kelly

The People Could Fly: American Black Folktales

Virginia Hamilton. *The People Could Fly: American Black Folktales.* Illustrated by Leo Dillon and Diane Dillon. New York: Alfred A. Knopf, 1985. ISBN 0-394-86925-7.

Suggested Grade Levels: 4–8

Plot Summary

This collection of twenty-four African American folktales includes a variety of stories written in different dialects. There are trickster tales with the wily Bruh Rabbit, tall tales, encounters with ghosts and devils, and stories of quests for freedom—from true slave narratives to fantasies with symbolic content. The author explains that in each case she has used "a reasonably colloquial language or dialect, depending on the folktale." The introduction and the explanations following the individual tales provide an understanding of the context of each story, detailing both the lives of the tellers and how the stories fit into the realm of traditional literature. This collection aptly demonstrates the importance of story in people's lives.

Teaching Suggestions

1. Children could compare one of these tales to another story-teller's version. For example, Hamilton's "Bruh Alligator Meets Trouble" could be compared to Julius Lester's "What's in Trouble?" in *The Knee-High Man.*

2. The tales could also be compared to variants found in different cultural contexts. For example, Hamilton's "Jack and the Devil" could be compared to Richard Chase's "Wicked John and the Devil" in *Grandfather Tales.*

3. Some tales could be compared to other works by Virginia Hamilton to examine how older folkloric character motifs can be reshaped by imagination into new stories. For instance, look at

the character John de Conquer in both "John and the Devil's Daughter" and *The Magical Adventures of Pretty Pearl.*

4. Children could create their own trickster tales or ghost stories using a character such as Brer Rabbit.

5. Children could select one tale and act it out using puppets or animal masks.

Related Books   Similar books of African American folklore:

Bang, Molly. *Wiley and the Hairy Man: Adapted from an American Folk Tale.*

Bryan, Ashley. *Lion and the Ostrich Chicks and Other African Tales.*

Bryan, Ashley. *Turtle Knows Your Name.*

Chase, Richard. *Grandfather Tales: American-English Folk Tales.*

Hamilton, Virginia. *The Magical Adventures of Pretty Pearl.*

Lester, Julius. *The Knee-High Man and Other Tales.*

Lester, Julius. *The Tales of Uncle Remus: The Adventures of Brer Rabbit.*

Lyons, Mary. *Raw Head, Bloody Bones: African-American Tales of the Supernatural.*

McKissack, Patricia. *Flossie and the Fox.*

McKissack, Patricia. *Mirandy and Brother Wind.*

—by Joan I. Glazer and Richard Van Dongen

Red Leaf, Yellow Leaf

Lois Ehlert. *Red Leaf, Yellow Leaf.* San Diego: Harcourt Brace Jovanovich, 1991. ISBN 0-15-266197-2.

Suggested Grade Levels: Preschool–2

Plot Summary

Blown free in the woods, twirling to the ground, the sugar maple seed sprouts, sinks its roots into the earth, and begins to grow. Soon the young tree is transplanted to a nursery, labeled and tended, measured and marked. When it is big enough, the tree is again uprooted, tied with twine, and delivered to another nursery, where it is chosen by a child for her very own. Each season provides a new and different reason to love and enjoy the tree.

Ehlert has created an exquisite textual collage for every page of this book. She has effectively incorporated seeds, roots, ribbons, nursery labels, twine, burlap, and other materials to enhance the reality of the tree and its journey from woods to lawn. Items in the illustrations, such as a suet bag, a round-pointed spade, and garden gloves, are neatly labeled. The final pages are devoted to illustrated definitions of such things as seeds, bark, and buds and to information necessary for successful tree planting, such as planting times, wrapping, and staking. The jacket even offers instructions on making a bird treat to hang in a tree.

Teaching Suggestions

1. As a class project, students could buy, plant, or adopt their own tree. This could include creating instructions for planting and tending the tree and charting the tree's growth and changes over a school year. Encourage children to write a story or poem incorporating information from their observations.

2. This book lends itself nicely to an extended study of the seasons or to a study of how the needs of plants change throughout the seasonal cycle. Students might incorporate real materials in an Ehlert-style collage to visually present some of what they learn.

3. Students could visit a nursery or garden center. Or they could invite a gardener to visit the class. Have students create a list of questions and explore ways to record the information.

4. Children could use real materials such as Ehlert does to create a class mural or their own books about a phenomenon they find intriguing.

Related Books   Other books that explore the theme of seasonal change:

Adoff, Arnold. *In for Winter, Out for Spring.*

Allison, Linda. *The Reasons for Seasons: The Great Cosmic Megagalactic Trip Without Moving from Your Chair.*

Aylesworth, Jim. *One Crow: A Counting Rhyme.*

Gibbons, Gail. *The Seasons of Arnold's Apple Tree.*

Lerner, Carol. *A Forest Year.*

Parnall, Peter. *Apple Tree.*

Watts, Barrie. *Apple Tree.*

Williams, John. *The Life Cycle of a Tree.*

Related books about trees:

Bash, Barbara. *Tree of Life: The World of the African Baobab.*

Behn, Harry. *Trees: A Poem.*

Burnie, David. *Tree.*

Cherry, Lynne. *The Great Kapok Tree: A Tale of the Amazon Rain Forest.*

Coats, Laura Jane. *The Oak Tree.*

Florian, Douglas. *Discovering Trees.*

Hiscock, Bruce. *The Big Tree.*

Jennings, Terry J. *Trees.*

Romanova, Natalia. *Once There Was a Tree.*

Ryder, Joanne. *Hello, Tree!*

Thomson, Ruth. *Trees.*

Udry, Janice May. *A Tree Is Nice.*

—by Rachael Hungerford

The Remembering Box

Eth Clifford. *The Remembering Box*. Illustrated by Donna Diamond. Boston: Houghton Mifflin, 1985. ISBN 0-395-38476-1.

Suggested Grade Levels: 3–5

Plot Summary

Nine-year-old Joshua has been spending the Sabbath with his Grandmother Goldina ever since he was five years old. He likes the traditional meals she prepares and finds the religious rituals they share satisfying. But the best thing about these weekend visits are the stories Grandma tells as she describes the events and people associated with the items and photographs in her "remembering box," which is an old trunk. On Joshua's last visit, when he is nearly ten, Grandma Goldina gives him a remembering box of his own and in it places a few of the special items. The family memories will then live on.

The many short episodes that Grandma Goldina relates to Joshua are intriguing stories in themselves and are told in an animated and amusing manner. This book as a whole exemplifies the importance of continuity within a family and a culture.

Teaching Suggestions

1. Children could use props from their own homes and families as starting points for telling or writing stories.

2. Family members, particularly grandparents, could be interviewed about special events, people, or stories that are part of the family's traditions. Have children retell or write these stories and collect them into a book.

3. The class might begin a "remembering box" for the year (or week or month) in school, adding items that have a special meaning or that are reminiscent of an event or person.

4. Children could construct a web of family or religious traditions they find satisfying.

Related Books

Other books that feature storytelling by older family members:

Bahr, Mary. *The Memory Box*.

Duke, Kate. *Aunt Isabel Tells a Good One.*

Farber, Norma. *How Does It Feel To Be Old?*

Fox, Mem. *Wilfrid Gordon McDonald Partridge.*

Howard, Elizabeth Fitzgerald. *Aunt Flossie's Hats (and Crab Cakes Later).*

Geras, Adele. *My Grandmother's Stories: A Collection of Jewish Folk Tales.*

Johnston, Angela. *Tell Me a Story, Mama.*

Jukes, Mavis. *Blackberries in the Dark.*

Lasky, Kathryn. *The Night Journey.*

Martin, Bill, Jr., and John Archambault. *Knots on a Counting Rope.*

Mathis, Sharon Bell. *The Hundred Penny Box.*

Orr, Katherine Shelley. *My Grandpa and the Sea.*

Wallace-Brodeur, Ruth. *Stories from the Big Chair.*

—by Joan I. Glazer

Return to Bitter Creek

Doris Buchanan Smith. *Return to Bitter Creek.* New York: Viking, 1986. ISBN 0-670-80783-4.

Suggested Grade Levels: 4–8

Plot Summary

Lacey, age twelve, her mother, Campbell, and her mother's boyfriend, David, come to the small Appalachian community in North Carolina where Campbell grew up and where her family still lives. In a series of tense encounters with various family members, Lacey finds herself caught between her resentment of their attempts to run her life and her desire to be a part of this extended family. Lacey grows to understand the needs and motivations that underlie the behavior of those around her. Strong characterization helps the reader to vicariously experience the tragedy that befalls this family.

Teaching Suggestions

1. Children could select one incident from the book and dramatize it. Encourage them to make notes about how their character feels about a situation and why; how their character might show his or her feelings in language, posture, or actions; and how these feelings are revealed in the book.

2. Have children write a diary entry for one character in the book describing a specific incident from that person's point of view. Classmates could tell whose diary they think it is and why.

3. Students might discuss the importance of names, beginning with the use of Campbell or Ann for Lacey's mother (p. 34), Lacey's grandfather's (p. 15) and Kenny's reaction (p. 19) to David Habib, and the use of Lacey or Lacey Ann and Mrs. and Ms. (p. 67).

4. After reading the book, children could reread the pages that describe the symbols on the quilt that Grandmom had made. They could then design a symbol to introduce each chapter. (Page 124 could be used as an introduction to symbolism.)

Related Books   Other books that feature troubled families in an Appalachian setting:

Armstrong, William H. *Sounder.*

Cleaver, Vera, and Bill Cleaver. *Where the Lilies Bloom.*

Little, Jean. *Mama's Going to Buy You a Mockingbird.*

MacLachlan, Patricia. *Journey.*

Paterson, Katherine. *Come Sing, Jimmy Jo.*

Rylant, Cynthia. *Missing May.*

Smith, Doris Buchanan. *The First Hard Times.*

Books that can give students a sense of the Appalachian region:

Anderson, Joan. *Pioneer Children of Appalachia.*

Rylant, Cynthia. *Appalachia: The Voices of Sleeping Birds.*

Hendershot, Judith. *In Coal Country.*

Lyon, George Ella. *Come a Tide.*

Lyon, George Ella. *A Regular Rolling Noah.*

O'Kelley, Mattie Lou. *From the Hills of Georgia: An Autobiography in Paintings.*

Rylant, Cynthia. *Best Wishes.*

Rylant, Cynthia. *Waiting to Waltz.*

Rylant, Cynthia. *When I Was Young in the Mountains.*

Smucker, Anna E. *No Star Nights.*

Other books about "changing" families:

Fine, Anne. *My War with Goggle-Eyes.*

Myers, Walter Dean. *The Mouse Rap.*

Pevsner, Stella. *Sister of the Quints.*

Slote, Alfred. *The Trading Game.*

—by Joan I. Glazer

Sarah, Plain and Tall

Patricia MacLachlan. *Sarah, Plain and Tall*. New York: Harper and Row, 1985. ISBN 0-06-024101-2.

Suggested Grade Levels: 3–6

Plot Summary

Anna and her younger brother Caleb are surprised then pleased when their father explains that he has advertised for a wife and has received a reply. Sarah Wheaton from Maine tells them through her letters that she is "plain and tall" and not "mild mannered." She arrives at their pioneer prairie home to spend a month to see if the marriage will work. The children love her immediately and hang on her every word and action, interpreting each as to whether she will stay or not. Told through Anna's eyes, this narrative is rich in descriptive language and understated meanings. The book is a richly deserved Newbery Medal winner.

Teaching Suggestions

1. Children could create the advertisement that the father might have written to entice Sarah to come.

2. While rereading MacLachlan's descriptions of the prairie and of Maine, ask the children to imagine what these landscapes look like. Encourage children to draw these scenes using blue, green, gray, and black colored pencils or crayons—the colors that Sarah brought. Have the children investigate informational books that describe the prairie and Maine landscapes to further their understanding of these environments.

3. Children could write a letter that Sarah might have written to her brother William at some point in the story, such as immediately upon her arrival, after the storm, or after her decision to stay.

4. Children could draw pictures as though they were snapshots in a photo album. They should decide which character has the camera and write a caption under each "photo."

5. Each character is richly described in the book. Have children keep an ongoing chart of words and phrases describing each major character. After concluding their reading, they could se-

lect one character and write a biographical sketch using the descriptions they've gathered from the book.

Related Books   Other excellent books on prairie life:

Anderson, Joan. *Christmas on the Prairie.*
Conrad, Pam. *Prairie Songs.*
Conrad, Pam. *Prairie Visions: The Life and Times of Solomon Butcher.*
Freedman, Russell. *Children of the Wild West.*
George, Jean Craighead. *One Day in the Prairie.*
Harvey, Brett. *Cassie's Journey: Going West in the 1860's.*
Harvey, Brett. *My Prairie Year: Based on the Diary of Elenore Plaisted.*
Nixon, Joan Lowery. *A Family Apart.*
Turner, Ann. *Dakota Dugout.*
Turner, Ann. *Grasshopper Summer.*
Wilder, Laura Ingalls. *Little House on the Prairie.*
Wilder, Laura Ingalls. *Little Town on the Prairie.*

Children might also like to read other books by MacLachlan and compare them to this one in terms of tone, style, characterization, and other elements:

Arthur, For the Very First Time
Cassie Binegar
The Facts and Fictions of Minna Pratt
Journey
Seven Kisses in a Row
Three Names
Through Grandpa's Eyes
Tomorrow's Wizard
Unclaimed Treasures

—by Joan I. Glazer

The Secret Language of Snow

Terry Tempest Williams and Ted Major. *The Secret Language of Snow*. Illustrated by Jennifer Dewey. San Francisco: Sierra Club/Pantheon Books, 1984. ISBN 0-394-86574-X.

Suggested Grade Levels: 2–7

Plot Summary

While most of us don't live in a world that is covered with snow "as far as the eye can see," the Inuits in the Far North do. As a result, the language they use to describe their snow is much more detailed than our language is. We may say "It's snowing" and mean that white stuff is falling to the ground. The Inuits, on the other hand, have words to distinguish the different ways snow can fall, the different qualities of snow, and the different places where snow can be found. For example, *annui* means falling snow; *api* means snow on the ground; *pukak* means snow that can cause avalanches; *qali* means snow that collects horizontally on trees; *upsik* means wind-beaten snow; *siqoq* means swirling or drifting snow; and *kimoagruk* means snow drift.

The Secret Language of Snow focuses on one group of Inuit people, the Kobuk. Besides describing various kinds of snow, the authors also reveal aspects of Kobuk culture, such as the importance of listening "in order to survive," of sharing stories in order "to pass on their knowledge and wisdom to the younger ones," and of singing to "lighten the days when winter traps the Kobuk people indoors." Scientific terms and knowledge are introduced along with practical, easy-to-understand examples. Black-and-white sketches help to explain the setting and terminology. A table of contents, a bibliography for further study, and a subject index are also included.

Teaching Suggestions

1. Locate where the Inuit people live on a map. Ask children to determine why they might have "snow as far as the eye can see."

2. Have children chart similarities and differences between Inuit children and themselves.

3. The authors suggest that good storytellers paint pictures with words. Have children find examples of this in the book. Then they could write a "painting" about a season in their area.

4. The people of the Far North use songs for hunting and controlling the weather. What are songs used for in your area? Children could find and play examples.

5. The class could try out some of the activities suggested by the authors, such as examining crystals (p. 42), tracks in the snow (p. 64), or snow patterns (p. 73); building a qalimeter (p. 81); making kanik or rime (p. 86); or building a snow shelter (p. 101).

6. The class might also make a list of things that someone would have to know or do in order to write a book like *The Secret Language of Snow.*

Related Books   Other books that use the Arctic as their focus:

Branley, Franklyn M. *Snow Is Falling.*

Ekoomiak, Normee. *Arctic Memories.*

George, Jean Craighead. *Julie of the Wolves.*

George, Jean Craighead. *One Day in the Alpine Tundra.*

Hiscock, Bruce. *Tundra: The Arctic Land.*

Houston, James. *Drifting Snow: An Arctic Search.*

Hoyt-Goldsmith, Diane. *Arctic Hunter.*

London, Jack. *Call of the Wild.*

Mayo, Gretchen. *Star Tales: North American Indian Stories about the Stars.*

Murphy, Claire Rudolf. *Friendship across Arctic Waters: Alaskan Cub Scouts Visit Their Soviet Neighbors.*

Stokes, Donald W. *A Guide to Nature in Winter: Northeast and North Central North America.*

—by Marilou R. Sorensen

Small Poems Again

Valerie Worth. *Small Poems Again.* Illustrated by Natalie Babbitt. New York: Farrar, Straus and Giroux, 1986. ISBN 0-374-37074-5.

Suggested Grade Levels: 3–8

Plot Summary

This is the fourth volume in a series of uncommon poems about common, everyday things. Worth's perfectly selected words make unique, pithy observations on everything from seashells and starfish to coat hangers and telephone poles. The images are fresh and creative. For example, asparagus spears are compared to "a nest / of snakes / awakened." Starfish are described as "spined / with sparks, / Limbed with flames, / climbing / the dark / To cling / And shine," while fleas are described as "Roaming these / Furry prairies" (referring to a dog's back). Babbitt's black-and-white line drawings simply yet perceptively depict each object.

Teaching Suggestions

1. After reading this book, have each child (or perhaps sets of partners) select a special object as the subject for a small poem. They should first illustrate that object carefully and in detail, brainstorm a list of words that specifically describe their object, and then use the drawings and lists to write a poem about it.

2. Take children on a nature walk, encouraging them to take special care in observing everything. They can then select one thing to write a poem about.

3. Have children make attribute lists in which they record their favorite descriptive phrases from this collection.

4. Poems such as "Amoeba," "Asparagus," and "Kaleidoscope" can be used in a guessing game format. Teachers or students could read a poem aloud, omitting the title. The class would then be asked to guess the object being described. This activity encourages children to listen closely and to think carefully about how Worth uses words.

5. Ask children to compare the poems in this collection to those in Worth's other collections (or to those in collections of similar poems; see related books). Make a class book of their favorites.

Related Books   Other books that feature short poetic observations of everyday objects:

Chandra, Deborah. *Balloons and Other Poems.*
Harrison, Michael. *Splinters: A Book of Very Short Poems.*
Janeczko, Paul B. *Postcard Poems: A Collection of Poetry for Sharing.*
McMillan, Bruce. *One Sun: A Book of Terse Verse.*
Worth, Valerie. *Small Poems.*
Worth, Valerie. *More Small Poems.*
Worth, Valerie. *Still More Small Poems.*
Worth, Valerie. *All the Small Poems.*

—by Amy McClure

The Spring of Butterflies and Other Folktales of China's Minority Peoples

He Liyi, translator. *The Spring of Butterflies and Other Folktales of China's Minority Peoples.* Edited by Neil Philip. Illustrated by Pan Aiqing and Li Zhao. New York: Lothrop, Lee and Shepard, 1986. ISBN 0-688-06192-3.

Suggested Grade Levels: 4 and up

Plot Summary

While students will be familiar with many of the situations and themes found in the fourteen tales of this anthology, the tales also reveal beliefs and values particular to some of the minority populations living in the various provinces of China. The tales contain recognizable story structures such as the quest (in "The Princess's Veil," "A Golden Fish," and "The Story of the Washing Horse Pond"), familiar plot devices such as the magical helper who provides assistance to those deserving of it (in "A Crane and Two Brothers" and "A Golden Fish"), and, of course, poetic justice (in "The Two Brothers" and "The Wonderful Brocade"). Yet woven into the tales—and often central to their unfolding—are details that provide at least some understanding of the distinctive temperament of the various cultures from which the tales derived.

Teaching Suggestions

1. Using both the information provided in the introduction to the anthology and the tales themselves, locate the province associated with each tale on a map of China.

2. Have students compare and contrast similar folktales in order to note variations in specific story elements. Once they are familiar with these details, lead them through the process of composing original tales based on the ones they have discussed. Teachers could focus on the following tales:

He's tales	Related tales	Dominant elements
"The Wonderful Brocade"	"The Water of Life"	Faithful son; quest
"The Tibetan Envoy"; "Never Heard of This Before"	"The Fool of the World and the Flying Ship" (in Cole)	Tested suitor
"The Dougarda Brothers"	"The Story of the Youth Who Went Forth to Learn What Fear Was" (in Yolen)	Unlikely hero
"A Woman's Love"	"Li Chi Slays the Serpent"; "Vassilisa the Beautiful" (in Yolen)	Likely heroine
"The Golden Fish"	"The Search for the Magic Lake" (in Cole)	Magical helper
"The Princess's Veil"	"The Forest Bride" (in Cole)	Least likely suitor

3. Students can focus on language style by comparing "The Wonderful Brocade" to Cole's version of the tale, "The Magical Brocade." Encourage further exploration of style by examining the information in the introduction concerning the decisions of editors and translators. For example, the introduction mentions He's "rhythmical felicity," "manipulation of sound," and unique, idiosyncratic wording. Find examples of these elements in particular tales in the anthology and discuss their effect on situation and character.

4. Teachers can extend student response to the tales with drama:

   a. Have pairs of students prepare a tableau that depicts the suitor's conflict with the witch in "The Princess's Veil." Invite the students to share their various interpretations of the incident, and have the characters in each tableau reveal their thoughts and feelings by directing them to come alive. Encourage the audience to suggest a caption for each tableau.

   b. Have the students work in small groups. One student is a tour guide; the others are tourists who are visiting the legendary spring that is the central element in "The Spring of Butterflies." The guide explains the details of the legend to this inquisitive group. After the tour, the visitors to the site write their impressions in their travel logs or journals.

    c. Using *Readers Theatre for Children* as a source, have the students work in small groups to prepare and present Readers Theatre scripts for their favorite passages in the tales.

5. Enrich the students' understanding of the tales with storytelling. Have them prepare storytelling presentations by focusing on significant incidents in the tales. Encourage different students to prepare some of the same incidents separately in order to stimulate discussion of the ways minor and major changes in inflection, gesture, eye contact, movement, and other storytelling techniques can alter interpretation and audience response.

Related Books

The following are excellent folktales to compare to those in this collection:

Cole, Joanna. *Best-Loved Folktales of the World.*

Rogasky, Barbara. *The Water of Life: A Tale from the Brothers Grimm.*

Yep, Laurence. *Child of the Owl.*

Yolen, Jane. *Favorite Folktales from Around the World.*

For an excellent resource for doing Readers Theatre with children, see Mildred Knight Laughlin and Kathy Howard Latrobe's *Readers Theatre for Children: Scripts and Script Development.* The book also includes folktales suitable for acting out.

—by Anthony L. Manna

The Talking Eggs: A Folktale from the American South

Robert D. San Souci. *The Talking Eggs: A Folktale from the American South.* Illustrated by Jerry Pinkney. New York: Dial Books, 1989. ISBN 0-8037-0619-7.

Suggested Grade Levels: 2–4

Plot Summary

This distinctly Creole folktale is about two daughters in the good sister/mean sister tradition. Rose is spoiled and lazy and doesn't "know beans from birds' eggs"; Blanche is "sweet and kind and sharp as forty crickets." The mother prefers Rose, who, like her, is "always putting on airs." All live on a farm poor enough to look "like the tail end of bad luck." One day Blanche sets off for a bucket of water, and as she returns she befriends an old woman. The old woman eventually leads her to her tumbledown shack, first extracting a promise that Blanche will not laugh at anything she sees. Of course, the woman's yard is filled with wonders, the most remarkable of which are talking eggs, some bejewelled, some plain, all vying for Blanche's attention. As instructed, Blanche takes only the plain eggs. The ending of the story is predictable and satisfying.

Pinkney's outstanding pencil and watercolor illustrations are vibrant and alive with expression, perfectly matching the text. His pictures are splashed with color and draw the reader into Blanche's world. This book was a Caldecott Medal honor book.

Teaching Suggestions

1. Character sketches of Blanche and Rose on giant-sized body outlines will encourage children to think about the differences between both girls. After brainstorming for adjectives that can be written on the outline, children can record snippets of text and episodes from the story to support their findings.

2. There are many folktales with the good sister/bad sister theme.

Children can read widely in this area and compare other versions. This tale was orally spread from Europe to Louisiana. How does this particular version compare to its European counterpart? What has been added or altered in this Creole version?

3. Language makes for fascinating study. Words and phrases unique to *The Talking Eggs* could be explored. For example, what does it mean to be as alike as two peas in a pod? to gawk? to be contrary? to hightail into the woods?

4. Share other Creole folktales. Have children compile a list of the unique characteristics of these tales.

5. Other books illustrated by Jerry Pinkney could be examined to begin drawing conclusions about his artistic style.

Related Books   Other excellent collections of African and African American folklore that could be compared to this one:

Aardema, Verna. *Rabbit Makes a Monkey of Lion: A Swahili Tale.* Illustrated by Jerry Pinkney.

Arkhurst, Joyce Cooper. *The Adventures of Spider: West African Folk Tales.* Illustrated by Jerry Pinkney.

Climo, Shirley. *The Egyptian Cinderella.*

Lester, Julius. *The Tales of Uncle Remus: The Adventures of Brer Rabbit.* Illustrated by Jerry Pinkney.

Lester, Julius. *More Tales of Uncle Remus: Further Adventures of Brer Rabbit, His Friends, Enemies, and Others.* Illustrated by Jerry Pinkney.

Because this is a Cinderella variant, students could compare this story to similar variants, such as John Steptoe's *Mufano's Beautiful Daughters: An African Tale, Moss Gown,* "The Indian Cinderella," *The Brocade Slipper, The Month-Brother, Tattercoats, Vassilisa the Beautiful, Yeh-Shen: A Cinderella Story from China,* and "Cenerentola" (an Italian version found in Virginia Haviland's *Favorite Fairy Tales Told in Italy*), as well as to Perrault's traditional version.

—by Susan Lehr

Tar Beach

Faith Ringgold. *Tar Beach.* New York: Crown Publishers, 1991.
ISBN 0-517-58030-6.

Suggested Grade Levels: 2–5

Plot Summary

"Flights of fancy" isn't a term to be taken lightly when used in reference to Cassie Louise Lightfoot. Cassie is eight years old, in the third grade, lives in New York, and can "fly"! Cassie spends her summer nights picnicking and dreaming on her "beach"—the tarred roof of her apartment building. There she uses her wonderfully vivid imagination to fly about the city, free to do and own what she wants for the rest of her life. She finds steady, safe work and status for her father, who can't join the union because of a "grandfather clause." She wears the sparkling George Washington Bridge (opened on the day she was born) as her own diamond necklace. And she teaches her brother Be Be to fly too, telling him that "all you need is somewhere to go that you can't get to any other way."

Tar Beach concerns the experience of black women in America. Cassie's dream of "flying free" to accomplish her dreams echoes the motif of flying free found in African American folktales, where it served as wish fulfillment and as metaphorical escape from slavery. The effect of the historical exclusion of minorities from unions and certain jobs on black and other minority families is also a strong thread in the story. But the author's vision of a black woman accomplishing bold, creative things comes through in "Cassie's power to emancipate her father." In combining storytelling, painting, and quilt-making in one unique art form, Faith Ringgold has created an exquisite picture book that won well-deserved Caldecott honors.

Teaching Suggestions

1. Children could explore the motif of "flying free" in a variety of African American folktales. Discussion of this and other motifs in traditional literature would expand their knowledge of the genre and of ethnic experiences.

2. This book could prompt further investigation of topics such as

work and living conditions during the Great Depression, the experiences of minorities at the time, and the meaning of terms such as "grandfather clause." This kind of work could involve discussion, finding historical reference materials, note-taking, conducting interviews of family and community members who lived and worked during the Depression, or writing and presenting reports of various kinds on related topics.

3. A final page in *Tar Beach* discusses how Faith Ringgold combines storytelling, painting, and quilt-making. Class members could create a quilt of their own that tells their own class or story history. In addition, the class might explore the history of quilt-making itself. Perhaps they could invite a quilt-maker to come and demonstrate the process.

4. *Double Stitch* is an adult book in which black women writers use the quilt as a metaphor to write about mothers and daughters. Yet it also contains a number of stories and poems that could be used effectively in elementary classrooms. The class could find and read aloud other stories that involve quilts or quilt-making and discuss the authors' use of the quilt as a metaphor.

5. Children could write and illustrate their own stories about "flying free."

Related Books

Other books that use quilt-making as a theme:

Bell-Scott, Patricia. *Double Stitch: Black Women Write about Mothers and Daughters.*

Coerr, Eleanor. *The Josefina Story Quilt.*

Flournoy, Valerie. *The Patchwork Quilt.*

Grifalconi, Ann. *Osa's Pride.*

Hamilton, Virginia. *The People Could Fly: Black American Folktales.*

Johnston, Tony. *The Quilt Story.*

Jonas, Ann. *The Quilt.*

Mills, Lauren. *The Rag Coat.*

Polacco, Patricia. *The Keeping Quilt.*

For a related book about the Brooklyn Bridge, see *The Brooklyn Bridge: They Said It Couldn't Be Built* by Judith St. George.

—by Rachael Hungerford

Thunder Cake

Patricia Polacco. *Thunder Cake.* New York: Philomel Books, 1990.
ISBN 0-399-22231-6.

Suggested Grade Levels: K–3

Plot Summary

On the opening page of this book, the author explains that as a child in Michigan she was afraid of the thunderstorms that rolled in on sultry summer days. This book is the story of how her grandmother—her "Babushka"—helped her overcome that fear. When the child hides under the bed upon hearing thunder, Babushka coaxes her out, explaining that when you see the lightning, you count until you hear the thunder. The number you end up with is the number of miles away the storm is from the house. This is important, for one has to know how far away the storm is in order to make Thunder Cake, which must be in the oven before the storm arrives. As a storm approaches, Babushka sends the child out to gather the ingredients for the cake: eggs from the hen house; milk from the cow; chocolate, sugar, and flour from the shed in the woods; and the secret ingredients—tomatoes and strawberries. Then they both mix up the cake and get it in the oven in time. Afterward, Babushka tells her granddaughter that "only a very brave person could have done all them things!" The story ends with child and grandmother enjoying the cake as the storm rages outside.

As in her other books, Polacco's illustrations are filled with the vivid colors and patterns of folk art. The use of talk and a warm adult-child relationship to calm fears make this book an excellent model to share with children.

Teaching Suggestions

1. Read the book aloud and invite the children's responses to the story as it unfolds. Young children like to count with the text and make the sound of thunder at the appropriate moment. A class of second graders listened to this story on a September day. That evening a heavy storm hit the area, and the children told stories the next day of counting between the lightning and thunder as a way of overcoming their fears.

2. Children might enjoy baking the Thunder Cake and sharing favorite family recipes. The book might also bring out stories of times with grandparents, of life in rural areas, or of ethnic clothing like Babushka's.

3. A teacher might raise the question as to why lightning and thunder are separated by a few seconds and help children seek out the answer.

4. Patricia Polacco has a distinctive artistic style that young children will quickly recognize. Other Polacco books could be shared to help children see similarities in both writing style and illustrations.

Related Books

Other books about overcoming fear of storms:

Martin, Bill, Jr., and John Archambault. *The Ghost-Eye Tree.*
Steig, William. *Brave Irene.*
Stolz, Mary. *Storm in the Night.*
Zolotow, Charlotte. *The Storm Book.*

Other books by Polacco that could be compared to this one:

Babushka's Doll
Just Plain Fancy
The Keeping Quilt
Mrs. Katz and Tush
Rechenka's Eggs

The High Rise Glorious Skittle Skat Roarious Sky Pie Angel Food Cake by Nancy Willard similarly features cake-baking, although for a different purpose.

—by Carol Avery

50 The True Confessions of Charlotte Doyle

Avi. *The True Confessions of Charlotte Doyle.* New York: Orchard Books, 1990. ISBN 0-531-05893-X.

Suggested Grade Levels: 4–8

Plot Summary

"Not every thirteen-year-old girl is accused of murder, brought to trial, and found guilty. But I was such a girl and my story is worth telling." Thus begins the story of Charlotte Doyle, who set sail from Liverpool, England, to join her family in America on June 16, 1832. The journal Charlotte kept on her trip allows her to retell her story many years later, and the details of her experience and the intensity of her emotions vividly bring the story to life. On the voyage to America, the crew revolts against the captain. Charlotte, who began the journey as a young lady and the captain's confidante, eventually joins the crew in this revolt.

All of this is skillfully handled by the author as he leads the reader through Charlotte's first-person narrative. The story is filled with suspense, and the ending, although somewhat controversial, is satisfying. An appendix includes drawings of a sailing ship and an explanation of ship's time. This book was a Newbery honor book for 1991.

Teaching Suggestions

1. This book naturally lends itself to studies of history because it provides glimpses of well-drawn fictional characters in authentic settings. Teachers could incorporate the book as one of many novels that document the early years of American history.

2. The book can also evoke many discussions about topics such as life on a sailing vessel, transportation in the early nineteenth century, and the role of women at the time. At the point in the story where Charlotte has returned to her home in Providence, invite students to write to Charlotte offering advice. Or they could write to her father, giving him their opinion of his ac-

tions. Students might also enjoy comparing the life of girls today to the life of those in the early nineteenth century.

3. Since the book is written as a journal, the value and process of writing a journal could be discussed. Use selected entries to demonstrate the usefulness of journals in helping people cope with difficult times or in thinking through important decisions. And since the author's style of writing reflects the writing of the period, students could compare Charlotte's writing to examples of first-person narratives set in twentieth-century America. Or they could keep their own journals of daily experiences for a week or two and compare their own styles to Charlotte's.

4. If this story is read aloud, a blown-up version of the labeled drawing of the sailing ship in the appendix could be posted for handy reference. Some students might want to learn more about the rigging and structure of various sailing ships by studying reference books or ship models. Students could build a model of the "Seahawk" or a part of the ship important to the story using the descriptions in the book and the illustrations found in the appendix.

5. Suspend reading aloud at the point where Charlotte is brought to trial. Assign parts and hold a mock trial. Evidence must come from information presented in the story.

6. Older students could compare the unusual format of this book to that of Avi's *Nothing But the Truth*, which is written as memos, conversations, newspaper articles, and other nontraditional forms. They might note how story is revealed through these forms in a manner different from that of traditional prose. Also invite students to read Avi's *The Man Who Was Poe* and to look for connections to *The True Confessions of Charlotte Doyle*. For example, the "Seahawk" is mentioned on page 129 of *The Man Who Was Poe*.

7. Charlotte's final decision will undoubtedly change her life. Students might be interested in speculating about how Charlotte's life might develop in different directions depending upon how she resolves this final dilemma. They could then make a detailed comparison of the "two lives of Charlotte Doyle," with one "life" determined by one decision and the other determined by the alternative.

8. Help to establish a mood by extending students' appreciation of the poetry, art, and music of the times. Students might enjoy "Old Ironsides" by Oliver Wendell Holmes and "The Wreck of the Hesperus" by Henry Wadsworth Longfellow. Find sea scenes

and drawings of sailing ships ("On a Lee Shore" by Winslow Homer, for example). Students might also enjoy music from Rodger's "Victory at Sea" or sea chanties (an idea from *Booklinks*, February 15, 1993, American Library Association).

Related Books

The following books also show young protagonists who find themselves in difficult situations and use their resourcefulness to resolve things:

Cleary, Beverly. *Strider.*

Fleischman, Paul. *Saturnalia.*

Fox, Paula. *The Slave Dancer.*

Gleeson, Libby. *Eleanor, Elizabeth.*

Hendry, Frances Mary. *Quest for a Maid.*

Hesse, Karen. *Letters from Rifka.*

Hudson, Jan. *Sweetgrass.*

Lasky, Kathryn. *Beyond the Divide.*

O'Dell, Scott. *Sarah Bishop.*

Paterson, Katherine. *Lyddie.*

Pullman, Philip. *The Ruby in the Smoke.*

Speare, Elizabeth George. *The Witch of Blackbird Pond.*

Books about life on the sea:

DePauw, Linda Grant. *Seafaring Women.*

Fisher, Leonard Everett. *The Shipbuilders.*

Loeper, John J. *The Golden Dragon: By Clipper Ship Around the Horn.*

O'Dell, Scott. *The Dark Canoe.*

Paulsen, Gary. *The Voyage of the Frog.*

Books in which characters use journals or diaries:

Avi. *The Man Who Was Poe.*

Avi. *Nothing But the Truth.*

Blos, Joan W. *A Gathering of Days: A New England Girl's Journal, 1830–32.*

Byars, Betsy. *The Burning Questions of Bingo Brown.*

Cameron, Eleanor. *The Private Worlds of Julia Redfern.*

Cleary, Beverly. *Dear Mr. Henshaw.*

Fisher, Leonard Everett. *The Death of Evening Star: The Diary of a Young New England Whaler.*

Glaser, Dianne. *The Diary of Trilby Frost.*
Paulsen, Gary. *The Island.*
Roop, Peter, and Connie Roop. *I, Columbus: My Journal, 1492–1493.*
Stevens, Carla. *A Book of Your Own: Keeping a Diary or Journal.*
Turner, Ann. *Nettie's Trip South.*

—by Carol Avery and Carl Tomlinson

Tuesday

David Wiesner. *Tuesday.* New York: Clarion Books, 1991.
ISBN 0-395-55113-7.

ISBN 0-395-55113-7.

Suggested Grade Levels: K–4

Plot Summary

On Tuesday evening, peacefully asleep on the pond, the frogs are surprised and delighted to find themselves aloft on flying lily pads. They quickly learn how to navigate laundry on the line, telephone wires, open windows, and large dogs. Then, as suddenly and unexpectedly as it began, the magic flight is over, leaving the frogs to hop home, tired and disgruntled. Yet the reader is left to anticipate the possibilities for next Tuesday. Sparse language and rollicking visual images contribute to the wonderful humor and anticipation of this Caldecott-winning story.

Teaching Suggestions

1. The scarcity of text in this book invites readers to retell or rewrite a more elaborate version of the story.

2. An ongoing writing possibility could be to create a book of "Tuesday" stories. Over the course of several Tuesdays, ordinary and unusual school events might be recorded and then transformed into magical adventures. Weekly observations of nature might also be transformed in a similar manner.

3. The many characters and actions in this book provide an opportunity for students to write a drama script for the story and present it to other classes or parents.

4. Wiesner's illustrations are indicative of the emotions of the various story characters: the frogs are obviously surprised, delighted, and then finally disgruntled; the humans are confused and curious; and the birds and the dogs are terrified. Such illustrations provide an excellent opportunity for discussion of feelings and how they are expressed wordlessly through the talent of the illustrator. Children might create lists of words and their own illustrations to express the feelings portrayed.

Related Books   Other books in which a character takes an unusual night journey:

Chesworth, Michael. *Rainy Day Dream.*
Grifalconi, Ann. *Darkness and the Butterfly.*
Howe, James. *I Wish I Were a Butterfly.*
Jonas, Ann. *The Trek.*
Keats, Ezra Jack. *The Trip.*
Ringgold, Faith. *Tar Beach.*
Wiesner, David. *Free Fall.*

Other "night books":

Aylesworth, Jim. *Country Crossing.*
Berger, Barbara. *Grandfather Twilight.*
Carlstrom, Nancy White. *Where Does the Night Hide?*
Denslow, Sharon Phillips. *Night Owls.*
Dragonwagon, Crescent. *Half a Moon and One Whole Star.*
Howard, Jane R. *When I'm Sleepy.*
Ichikawa, Satomi. *Nora's Stars.*
Rice, Eve. *Goodnight, Goodnight.*
Rylant, Cynthia. *Night in the Country.*
Wolff, Ashley. *Only the Cat Saw.*

—by Rachael Hungerford

Waiting to Waltz: A Childhood

Cynthia Rylant. *Waiting to Waltz: A Childhood.* Illustrated by
Stephen Gammell. Scarsdale, NY: Bradbury Press, 1984.
ISBN 0-02-778000-7.

Suggested Grade Levels: 5–8

Plot Summary

In thirty free verse poems that depict the precarious transition from childhood to adolescence, Rylant explores little moments of pleasure, longing, and wonder as they unfold in a small rural town. Rylant's poems demonstrate how a poet can observe, crystalize, and make universal the commonplace experiences of childhood. These accessible poems are excellent models for writers in the upper elementary grades.

Teaching Suggestions

1. Children could share their responses to the poems in dialogue journals with their peers. As a group, they could then determine which poems seem to reflect their feelings and situations most.

2. Students could independently read and annotate Cynthia Rylant's many fine books. Then they could create a classroom bibliography and distribute it to others through their school library.

3. Each child could pick a poem and analyze its use of descriptive words to create a sense of reality, mood, and setting. If two children pick the same poem, they could compare their work and determine why the poem is appealing to both of them.

4. Children could be encouraged to keep a poetry journal in which they copy their favorite poems, write their own, or keep phrases that catch their attention or imagination.

5. Children could write poems that capture significant events in their own lives.

Related Books   Other excellent poetry collections that explore the theme of growing into adolescence:

Adoff, Arnold. *Sports Pages.*
Carlson, Jo. *The Me Nobody Knows.*
Giovanni, Nikki. *Spin a Soft Black Song: Poems for Children.*
Glenn, Mel. *Class Dismissed! High School Poems.*
Glenn, Mel. *Class Dismissed II: More High School Poems.*
Holman, Felice. *The Song in My Head.*
Janeczko, Paul B. *Going Over to Your Place: Poems for Each Other.*
Mathis, Sharon Bell. *Red Dog, Blue Fly: Football Poems.*
Merriam, Eve. *A Sky Full of Poems.*
Rylant, Cynthia. *Soda Jerk.*

—by Anthony L. Manna and Jill P. May

The Wall

Eve Bunting. *The Wall*. Illustrated by Ronald Himler. New York: Clarion Books, 1990. ISBN 0-395-51588-2.

Suggested Grade Levels: All ages

Plot Summary

Through the voice of a young boy, Bunting presents the story of a visit to the Vietnam Veterans Memorial. "This is the wall, my grandfather's wall. On it are the names of those killed in a war, long ago," says the boy as he begins his story. The boy and his father search for the grandfather's name. A man without legs, sitting in a wheelchair, talks to the boy, and an old couple weeps in each other's arms. Then the boy and his father find the grandfather's name and make a rubbing of it. Each person seems touched in some way by the haunting site. After the story, Bunting includes a brief note of explanation about the Vietnam Veterans Memorial in Washington, D.C.

This moving story is notable for its recounting of the Vietnam story from a child's point of view. The prose is simple but never cloying. Himler's luminous watercolors capture the stark simplicity of the wall as well as the reactions of those who visit it.

Teaching Suggestions

1. A kindergarten teacher reported that after having read this book to her class, children requested that she read it again every day for two weeks. Read aloud, the book can open a discussion about war and peace with any age group.

2. A teacher might use this book to lead young readers to books by Eve Bunting on other social issues, including *How Many Days to America? A Thanksgiving Story*, a story of Cambodian people coming to America, and *Fly Away Home*, the story of a homeless boy and his father who live in an airport.

3. This book can be a resource for a social studies unit on twentieth-century history with a focus on war. The Vietnam War could be compared to Operation Desert Storm to help students understand how our country responded to both conflicts.

4. Students could interview veterans and other people in their community about life in combat and at home during the Vietnam War. These stories could then be compiled into a book.

Related Books   The following are a few of the many excellent books that also address the theme of war and peace:

Bunting, Eve. *Terrible Things: An Allegory of the Holocaust.*

Coerr, Eleanor. *Sadako and the Thousand Paper Cranes.*

Durrell, Ann, and Marilyn Sachs. *The Big Book for Peace.*

Gallaz, Christophe, and Roberto Innocenti. *Rose Blanche.*

Lyon, George Ella. *Cecil's Story.*

Maruki, Toshi. *Hiroshima No Pika.*

Morimoto, Junko. *My Hiroshima.*

Myers, Walter Dean. *Fallen Angels.*

Near, Holly. *The Great Peace March.*

Nelson, Theresa. *And One for All.*

Ray, Deborah Kogan. *My Daddy Was a Soldier: A World War II Story.*

Scholes, Katherine. *Peace Begins with You.*

Tsuchiya, Yukio. *Faithful Elephants: A True Story of Animals, People, and War.*

Wahl, Jan. *How the Children Stopped the Wars.*

Other books about the Vietnam Veterans Memorial:

Ashabranner, Brent K. *Always to Remember: The Story of the Vietnam Veterans Memorial.*

Donnelly, Judy. *A Wall of Names: The Story of the Vietnam Veterans Memorial.*

Wright, David K. *The Story of the Vietnam Memorial.*

Other books about the Vietnam War:

Hahn, Mary Downing. *December Stillness.*

Hauptly, Denis J. *In Vietnam.*

Paterson, Katherine. *Park's Quest.*

—by Carol Avery

We're Going on a Bear Hunt

Michael Rosen. *We're Going on a Bear Hunt.* Illustrated by Helen Oxenbury. New York: Margaret K. McElderry Books, 1989. ISBN 0-689-50476-4.

Suggested Grade Levels: Preschool–2

Plot Summary

The old story-song comes to life as a typical Oxenbury Dad sets out on a bear hunt with his four children and the family dog. This familiar children's favorite is most remembered by the refrain "We can't go over it. We can't go under it. Oh, No! We've got to go through it!" Oxenbury has effectively used double-page spreads with black-and-white sketches and watercolor paintings to convey the family's pleasure in their shared adventure and their encounters with grass, river, mud, forest, snow, and the "narrow, gloomy cave." Young readers will be attracted by the rhythm of Rosen's text, and they will discover that some new sounds accompany the memorable refrain—"squelch squerch" through the mud, "stumble trip" through the forest. Dramatically, the family moves "Tiptoe! Tiptoe!" into the bear's dark cave. The frightfully fun encounter sets the family on their nonstop return trip back through—in reverse order, of course—snowstorm, forest, mud, river, and grass to home, remembering to lock the door and heading for the safety of bed. After their escape, the family vows, "We're not going on a bear hunt again."

Teaching Suggestions

1. This book invites teachers to make a classroom bear hunt game in which players encounter the same obstacles that the family does. The game could be constructed according to the age and cognitive development of the children.

2. Young children could act out the sounds heard and situations described in the book using hand motions or dramatization.

3. In either oral or written form, children could imagine what

obstacles, situations, or encounters they might face while going on their own bear hunt.

4. Teachers could create a chart of the descriptive words used in the book. Then the children could add some new ones of their own.

Related Books

Other excellent bear-themed picture books:

Alborough, Jez. *Where's My Teddy?*

Barton, Byron. *The Three Bears.*

Brett, Jan. *Berlioz the Bear.*

Brett, Jan. *Goldilocks and the Three Bears.*

Degan, Bruce. *Jamberry.*

Fox, Mem. *Koala Lou.*

Freeman, Don. *Corduroy.*

Goldstein, Bobbye S. *Bear in Mind: A Book of Bear Poems.*

Kennedy, Jimmy. *Teddy Bears' Picnic.*

Langstaff, John M. *Oh, A-Hunting We Will Go.*

Minarik, Else Holmelund. *Little Bear.*

Marshall, James. *Goldilocks and the Three Bears.*

Martin, Bill, Jr., and John Archambault. *Brown Bear, Brown Bear, What Do You See?*

Schoenherr, John. *Bear.*

Siewert, Margaret, and Kathleen Savage. *Bear Hunt.*

Tolhurst, Marilyn. *Somebody and the Three Blairs.*

Yolen, Jane. *The Three Bears Rhyme Book.*

I'm Going on a Dragon Hunt by Maurice Jones uses the same pattern but has dragons as the focus.

—by Darwin L. Henderson

Whiskers and Rhymes

Arnold Lobel. *Whiskers and Rhymes.* New York: Greenwillow Books, 1985. ISBN 0-688-03835-2.

Suggested Grade Levels: K–2

Plot Summary

These original nursery rhymes about cats will delight the ear and tickle the imagination. Clever and witty, with illustrations to match, their language begs to be repeated.

Teaching Suggestions

1. Children could add motions to a selected rhyme, deciding how to interpret the action in each line and then teaching their interpretation to classmates.

2. First or second graders could compare some of the rhymes in this collection to ones they know from Mother Goose. What comes to mind, for example, when they read Lobel's "My London Bridge," "Sing a Song of Succotash," or "Gaily Afloat"?

3. Several of the rhymes, such as "Postman, Postman" and "Twinkle Toes," lend themselves to dramatization and Readers Theatre. Small groups could plan and present performances.

4. Rhymes such as "Sing, Sing" could be put on chart paper and used for choral reading. This poem in particular has a question-and-answer format and would work well with two groups of children.

5. Compare Lobel's collection of rhymes to other collections, some of which are listed below. After exploring common elements among a range of rhymes, encourage children to create rhymes of their own.

6. Discuss how illustrations can add to the humor and meaning of rhymes. Examine Lobel's illustrations as well as the illustrations in Wallace Tripp's *Granfa' Grig Had a Pig and Other Rhymes Without Reason.* Select a favorite rhyme and have children illustrate it. Compare and discuss the range of interpretations.

Related Books

The following are additional examples of unusual nursery rhyme collections:

Cousins, Lucy. *The Little Dog Laughed and Other Nursery Rhymes.*

Lee, Dennis. *Jelly Belly: Original Nursery Rhymes.*

Marshall, James. *James Marshall's Mother Goose.*

Schwartz, Amy, and Leonard S. Marcus. *Mother Goose's Little Misfortunes.*

Tripp, Wallace. *Granfa' Grig Had a Pig and Other Rhymes Without Reason.*

Watson, Clyde. *Catch Me and Kiss Me and Say It Again.*

Watson, Clyde. *Father Fox's Pennyrhymes.*

Nancy Larrick's *Cats Are Cats* is another good collection of poems about cats that could be compared to this one.

—by Joan I. Glazer

The Winter Room

Gary Paulsen. *The Winter Room.* New York: Orchard Books, 1989.
ISBN 0-531-05839-5.

Gary Paulsen. *The Winter Room.* New York: Orchard Books, 1989.
ISBN 0-531-05839-5.

Suggested Grade Levels: 4–8

Plot Summary

Eldon lives on a farm in northern Minnesota during the 1930s
with his older brother Wayne, his parents, and two older men,
Uncle David and Nels. Eldon takes the reader through the seasons
of life on the farm with all of its sights, sounds, and smells. In the
spring, the cows need to be pushed out from the muck behind the
barn, and the boys teach the new calves to drink out of a bucket,
read a Zane Grey western, and play at being cowboys. Summer is
filled with raising and harvesting crops. Fall brings butchering, a
time which Eldon dislikes. Winter is a time that "stands alone";
the household spends the cold nights around the stove, and Uncle
David tells stories from the family's Scandinavian heritage.

This book demonstrates Paulsen's gift of using words to create scenes involving all of the reader's senses. The vivid portrayal
of farm life through vignettes reveals the relationship among the
characters and clearly shows what life used to be like on an iso-
lated northern Minnesota farm. The outstanding language and
characterization of this book made it a Newbery Medal honor
book.

Teaching Suggestions

1. Students might compare farm life in the 1930s to farm life
   today and discuss the changes in the lives of farm families,
   their effect on American culture, and the disappearance of the
   family farm. George Ancona's *The American Family Farm* would
   be a helpful book to share during this activity.

2. In the book's introduction, Paulsen describes how authors create
   images. Students might discuss the introduction by considering
   the relationship between reader, writer, and text and the meaning of a reader's response.

3. Students could talk about the role of family storytelling in their
   own lives and share some of their stories.

4. Paulsen quietly creates conflict in the book, conflict that slowly builds to a confrontation and eventual resolution. Older readers could map this story structure and discuss how the author has created it.

Related Books

Other books about farming and farm life:

Ancona, George. *The American Family Farm.*

Azarian, Mary. *A Farmer's Alphabet.*

Bial, Raymond. *Corn Belt Harvest.*

Locker, Thomas. *Family Farm.*

McPhail, David M. *Farm Morning.*

Parnall, Peter. *Winter Barn.*

Peck, Robert Newton. *A Day No Pigs Would Die.*

Rylant, Cynthia. *Night in the Country.*

Siebert, Diane. *Heartland.*

Students could also compare this book to others by Paulsen.

—by Carol Avery

Woodsong

Gary Paulsen. *Woodsong*. Illustrated by Ruth Wright Paulsen. New York: Bradbury Press, 1990. ISBN 0-02-770221-9.

Suggested Grade Levels: 4–8

Plot Summary

Paulsen opens this autobiographical book with an incident that marked a change in his attitude about nature and life in the woods. While running his dogs on a crisp, beautiful December morning, he witnessed the kill of a doe by a pack of wolves. Paulsen explains at the end of the first chapter, "I began to understand that they are not wrong or right—they just are . . . it was wrong to think they should be the way I wanted them to be." In the next chapters, Paulsen describes other events: a confrontation with a bear during which the bear could have easily killed him but did not, coming upon a deer standing frozen to death in the snow, and the "summer of terror" when a banty hen ruled the roost and their yard as she defended her brood. Paulsen's relationship with his dogs and all they taught him provide the background for the book. The final chapters are journal entries from his seventeen-day run of the Iditarod in Alaska.

Paulsen's compelling, direct writing style draws the reader into the story. The descriptions of life in the wilderness are fascinating and evoke its mystique.

Teaching Suggestions

1. Paulsen's books are high-interest reading material. A sixth grader who read *Woodsong* tucked this note inside the cover: "I love Gary Paulsen's *Woodsong*. It was marvelous. I finished it in three hours." Children could keep a journal of the emotions they experience as the story progresses.

2. Readers may want to investigate the Iditarod, map its course, and learn about the winners and the strategies they used to accomplish their goal. Paulsen's experiences in the Iditarod could be compared to Bright Dawn's experiences in Scott O'Dell's *Black Star, Bright Dawn*.

3. *Woodsong* could open discussions about gun control and hunting. In a rural community where hunting is a way of life, this book prompted a lively discussion about these issues.

4. Have students read Paulsen's novel *Dogsong* and compare it to the autobiographical *Woodsong*. Discuss how the writing style differs between these two books.

5. Encourage students to explore other autobiographical writings (see the list below) and compare the different ways in which authors write about their lives.

6. Readers could discuss Paulsen's evolution as a writer after reading several of his books, focusing particularly on how his life experiences have shaped his writing.

Related Books

Other books that feature biographical or autobiographical accounts of authors' lives:

Byars, Betsy. *The Moon and I.*

Cleary, Beverly. *A Girl From Yamhill: A Memoir.*

Dorsett, Lyle, and Marjorie Mead. *C. S. Lewis Letters to Children.*

Fox, Mem. *Dear Mem Fox.*

Fritz, Jean. *Homesick: My Own Story.*

Gallo, Donald R. *Speaking for Ourselves: Autobiographical Sketches by Notable Authors of Books for Young Adults.*

Gallo, Donald R. *Speaking for Ourselves Too: Autobiographical Sketches by Notable Authors of Books for Young Adults.*

Greenfield, Eloise, and Lessie Jones Little. *Childtimes: A Three-Generation Memoir.*

Hyman, Trina Schart. *Self-Portrait: Trina Schart Hyman.*

Janeczko, Paul B. *The Place My Words Are Looking For: What Poets Say About and Through Their Work.*

Little, Jean. *Little by Little: A Writer's Education.*

Martin, Rafe. *A Storyteller's Story.*

Meltzer, Milton. *Starting from Home: A Writer's Beginnings.*

Naylor, Phyllis Reynolds. *How I Came To Be a Writer.*

Peet, Bill. *Bill Peet: An Autobiography.*

Rylant, Cynthia. *Best Wishes.*

Rylant, Cynthia. *But I'll Be Back Again: An Album.*

Stevenson, James. *When I Was Nine.*
Yolen, Jane. *A Letter from Phoenix Farm.*

After reading this autobiographical book, students might want to read other books by Paulsen.

—by Carol Avery

Bibliography of Notable Books

Adkins, Jan. 1985. *Workboats.* New York: Charles Scribner's Sons. ISBN 0-684-18228-9.

Adler, David. 1983. *Bunny Rabbit Rebus.* Illustrated by Madelaine Gill Linden. New York: Thomas Y. Crowell. ISBN 0-690-04196-9.

Adoff, Arnold. 1990. *In for Winter, Out for Spring.* Illustrated by Jerry Pinkney. San Diego: Harcourt Brace Jovanovich. ISBN 0-15-238637-8.

Ahlberg, Janet, and Allan Ahlberg. 1986. *The Jolly Postman; or, Other People's Letters.* Boston: Little, Brown. ISBN 0-316-02036-2.

Alborough, Jez. 1992. *Where's My Teddy?* Cambridge, MA: Candlewick Press. ISBN 1-56402-048-7.

Aliki. 1986. *How a Book Is Made.* New York: Thomas Y. Crowell. ISBN 0-690-04496-8.

————. 1989. *The King's Day: Louis XIV of France.* New York: Thomas Y. Crowell. ISBN 0-690-04590-5.

Anderson, Joan. 1985. *Christmas on the Prairie.* Photographs by George Ancona. New York: Clarion Books. ISBN 0-89919-307-2.

Andrews, Jan. 1986. *Very Last First Time.* Illustrated by Ian Wallace. New York: Atheneum. ISBN 0-689-50388-1.

Anno, Mitsumasa. 1983. *Anno's U.S.A.* New York: Philomel Books. ISBN 0-399-20974-3.

————. 1989. *Anno's Aesop: A Book of Fables by Aesop and Mr. Fox.* New York: Orchard Books. ISBN 0-531-05774-7.

Arnosky, Jim. 1992. *Otters Under Water.* New York: G. P. Putnam's Sons. ISBN 0-399-22339-8.

Avi. 1989. *The Man Who Was Poe.* New York: Orchard Books. ISBN 0-531-05833-6.

————. 1990. *The True Confessions of Charlotte Doyle.* New York: Orchard Books. ISBN 0-531-05893-X.

————. 1991. *Nothing But the Truth: A Documentary Novel.* New York: Orchard Books. ISBN 0-531-05959-6.

Aylesworth, Jim. 1992. *Old Black Fly.* Illustrated by Stephen Gammell. New York: Henry Holt. ISBN 0-8050-1401-2.

Babbitt, Natalie. 1987. *The Devil's Other Storybook: Stories and Pictures.* New York: Farrar, Straus and Giroux. ISBN 0-374-31767-4.

Baker, Keith. 1988. *The Dove's Letter.* San Diego: Harcourt Brace Jovanovich. ISBN 0-15-224133-7.

Barrett, Judi. 1983. *A Snake Is Totally Tail.* Illustrated by L. S. Johnson. New York: Atheneum. ISBN 0-689-30979-1.

Base, Graeme. 1987. *Animalia.* New York: Harry N. Abrams. ISBN 0-8109-1868-4.

———. 1989. *The Eleventh Hour: A Curious Mystery.* New York: Harry N. Abrams. ISBN 0-8109-0851-4.

Baylor, Byrd. 1983. *The Best Town in the World.* Illustrated by Ronald Himler. New York: Charles Scribner's Sons. ISBN 0-684-18035-9.

———. 1986. *I'm in Charge of Celebrations.* Illustrated by Peter Parnall. New York: Charles Scribner's Sons. ISBN 0-684-18579-2.

Bedard, Michael. 1992. *Emily.* Illustrated by Barbara Cooney. New York: Doubleday. ISBN 0-385-30697-0.

Beisner, Monika. 1983. *Monika Beisner's Book of Riddles.* New York: Farrar, Straus and Giroux. ISBN 0-374-30866-7.

Benjamin, Carol Lea. 1985. *Writing for Kids.* New York: Thomas Y. Crowell. ISBN 0-690-04490-9.

Bial, Raymond. 1991. *Corn Belt Harvest.* Boston: Houghton Mifflin. ISBN 0-395-56234-1.

Bierhorst, John. 1986. *The Monkey's Haircut and Other Stories Told by the Maya.* Illustrated by Robert Andrew Parker. New York: William Morrow. ISBN 0-688-04269-4.

———. 1987. *Doctor Coyote: A Native American Aesop's Fables.* Illustrated by Wendy Watson. New York: Macmillan. ISBN 0-02-709780-3.

Birdseye, Tom. 1988. *Airmail to the Moon.* Illustrated by Stephen Gammell. New York: Holiday House. ISBN 0-8234-0683-0.

Brittain, Bill. 1983. *The Wish Giver: Three Tales of Coven Tree.* New York: Harper and Row. ISBN 0-06-020686-1.

———. 1987. *Dr. Dredd's Wagon of Wonders.* Illustrated by Andrew Glass. New York: Harper and Row. ISBN 0-06-020713-2.

Brooks, Bruce. 1991. *Nature by Design.* New York: Farrar, Straus and Giroux. ISBN 0-374-30334-7.

Bruchac, Joseph, and Jonathan London. 1992. *Thirteen Moons on a Turtle's Back: A Native American Year of Moons.* Illustrated by Thomas Locker. New York: Philomel Books. ISBN 0-399-22141-7.

Bryan, Ashley. 1985. *The Cat's Purr.* New York: Atheneum. ISBN 0-689-31086-2.

Bunting, Eve. 1989. *The Wednesday Surprise.* Illustrated by Donald Carrick. New York: Clarion Books. ISBN 0-89919-721-3.

———. 1990. *The Wall.* Illustrated by Ronald Himler. New York: Clarion Books. ISBN 0-395-51588-2.

Burkert, Nancy Ekholm. 1989. *Valentine and Orson.* New York: Farrar, Straus and Giroux. ISBN 0-374-38078-3.

Byars, Betsy. 1988. *The Burning Questions of Bingo Brown.* New York: Viking. ISBN 0-670-81932-8.

Cameron, Ann. 1988. *The Most Beautiful Place in the World.* Illustrated by Thomas B. Allen. New York: Alfred A. Knopf. ISBN 0-394-89463-4.

Cameron, Eleanor. 1988. *The Private Worlds of Julia Redfern.* New York: E. P. Dutton. ISBN 0-525-44394-0.

Carlstrom, Nancy White. 1987. *Wild, Wild Sunflower Child Anna.* New York: Macmillan. ISBN 0-02-717360-7.

———. 1991. *Goodbye, Geese.* Illustrated by Ed Young. New York: Philomel Books. ISBN 0-399-21832-7.

Chandra, Deborah. 1990. *Balloons and Other Poems.* Illustrated by Leslie Bowman. New York: Farrar, Straus and Giroux. ISBN 0-374-30509-9.

Cleary, Beverly. 1983. *Dear Mr. Henshaw.* Illustrated by Paul O. Zelinsky. New York: William Morrow. ISBN 0-688-02405-X.

Clifford, Eth. 1985. *The Remembering Box.* Illustrated by Donna Diamond. Boston: Houghton Mifflin. ISBN 0-395-38476-1.

Cole, Brock. 1989. *Celine.* New York: Farrar, Straus and Giroux. ISBN 0-374-31234-6.

Cole, Joanna. 1990. *The Magic School Bus: Lost in the Solar System.* Illustrated by Bruce Degen. New York: Scholastic. ISBN 0-590-41428-3.

Coltman, Paul. 1985. *Tog the Ribber; or, Granny's Tale.* Illustrated by Gillian McClure. New York: Farrar, Straus and Giroux. ISBN 0-374-37630-1.

Conrad, Pam. 1990. *Stonewords: A Ghost Story.* New York: Harper and Row. ISBN 0-06-021316-7.

Craven, Carolyn. 1987. *What the Mailman Brought.* Illustrated by Tomie dePaola. New York: G. P. Putnam's Sons. ISBN 0-399-21290-6.

Cummings, Pat. 1992. *Talking with Artists.* New York: Bradbury Press. ISBN 0-02-724245-5.

Day, Alexandra. 1988. *Frank and Ernest.* New York: Scholastic. ISBN 0-590-41557-3.

———. 1990. *Frank and Ernest Play Ball.* New York: Scholastic. ISBN 0-590-42548-X.

DeFelice, Cynthia. 1988. *The Strange Night Writing of Jessamine Colter.* New York: Macmillan. ISBN 0-02-726451-3.

Deming, Alhambra G. 1988. *Who Is Tapping at My Window?* Illustrated by Monica Wellington. New York: E. P. Dutton. ISBN 0-525-44383-5.

dePaola, Tomie. 1983. *Sing, Pierrot, Sing: A Picture Book in Mime.* San Diego: Harcourt Brace Jovanovich. ISBN 0-15-274988-8.

de Regniers, Beatrice Schenk. 1985. *So Many Cats!* Illustrated by Ellen Weiss. New York: Clarion Books. ISBN 0-89919-322-6.

Detz, Joan. 1986. *You Mean I Have to Stand Up and Say Something?* Illustrated by David Marshall. New York: Atheneum. ISBN 0-689-31221-0.

Dewey, Jennifer. 1986. *Clem: The Story of a Raven.* New York: Dodd, Mead. ISBN 0-396-08728-0.

Domanska, Janina. 1985. *Busy Monday Morning.* New York: Greenwillow Books. ISBN 0-688-03833-6.

Dorris, Michael. 1992. *Morning Girl.* New York: Hyperion Books. ISBN 1-56282-284-5.

Dorsett, Lyle W., and Marjorie Lamp Mead. 1985. *C. S. Lewis Letters to Children.* New York: Macmillan. ISBN 0-02-570830-9.

Dragonwagon, Crescent. 1987. *Alligator Arrived with Apples: A Potluck Alphabet Feast.* Illustrated by Jose Aruego and Ariane Dewey. New York: Macmillan. ISBN 0-02-733090-7.

———. 1990. *Home Place.* Illustrated by Jerry Pinkney. New York: Macmillan. ISBN 0-02-733190-3.

Duncan, Lois. 1985. *Horses of Dreamland.* Illustrated by Donna Diamond. Boston: Little, Brown. ISBN 0-316-19554-5.

Edwards, Patricia. 1987. *Chester and Uncle Willoughby.* Illustrated by Diane Worfolk Allison. Boston: Little, Brown. ISBN 0-316-21173-7.

Ehlert, Lois. 1989. *Eating the Alphabet: Fruits and Vegetables from A to Z.* San Diego: Harcourt Brace Jovanovich. ISBN 0-15-224435-2.

———. 1990. *Feathers for Lunch.* San Diego: Harcourt Brace Jovanovich. ISBN 0-15-230550-5.

———. 1991. *Red Leaf, Yellow Leaf.* San Diego: Harcourt Brace Jovanovich. ISBN 0-15-266197-2.

Ekoomiak, Normee. 1990. *Arctic Memories.* New York: Henry Holt. ISBN 0-8050-1254-0.

Esbensen, Barbara. 1992. *Who Shrank My Grandmother's House? Poems of Discovery.* Illustrated by Eric Beddows. New York: HarperCollins. ISBN 0-06-021827-4.

Fields, Julia. 1988. *The Green Lion of Zion Street.* Illustrated by Jerry Pinkney. New York: Margaret K. McElderry Books. ISBN 0-689-50414-4.

Fisher, Leonard Everett. 1985. *Symbol Art: Thirteen Squares, Circles, Triangles from Around the World.* New York: Four Winds Press. ISBN 0-387-15203-2.

Fleischman, Paul. 1985. *Coming-and-Going Men: Four Tales.* Illustrated by Randy Gaul. New York: Harper and Row. ISBN 0-06-021883-5.

———. 1985. *I Am Phoenix: Poems for Two Voices.* Illustrated by Eric Beddows. New York: Harper and Row. ISBN 0-06-021881-9.

———. 1988. *Joyful Noise: Poems for Two Voices.* Illustrated by Eric Beddows. New York: Harper and Row. ISBN 0-06-021852-5.

———. 1990. *Saturnalia.* New York: Harper and Row. ISBN 0-06-021913-0.

———. 1991. *The Borning Room.* New York: HarperCollins. ISBN 0-06-023762-7.

———. 1992. *Townsend's Warbler.* New York: HarperCollins. ISBN 0-06-021874-6.

Fleming, Denise. 1991. *In the Tall, Tall Grass.* New York: Henry Holt. ISBN 0-8050-1635-X.

Fox, Mem. 1987. *Hattie and the Fox.* Illustrated by Patricia Mullins. New York: Bradbury Press. ISBN 0-02-735470-9.

———. 1989. *Night Noises.* Illustrated by Terry Denton. San Diego: Harcourt Brace Jovanovich. ISBN 0-15-200543-9.

Fox, Paula. 1984. *One-Eyed Cat.* Scarsdale, NY: Bradbury Press. ISBN 0-02-735540-3.

Frasier, Debra. 1991. *On the Day You Were Born.* San Diego: Harcourt Brace Jovanovich. ISBN 0-15-257995-8.

Furlong, Monica. 1991. *Juniper.* New York: Alfred A. Knopf. ISBN 0-394-83220-5.

Gallaz, Christophe. 1985. *Rose Blanche.* Illustrated by Roberto Innocenti. Mankato, MN: Creative Education, Inc. ISBN 0-87191-994-X.

Gardner, Beau. 1984. *The Look Again, and Again, and Again, and Again Book.* New York: Lothrop, Lee and Shepard. ISBN 0-688-03805-0.

Gay, Marie-Louise. 1989. *Rainy Day Magic.* Morton Grove, IL: Albert Whitman. ISBN 0-8075-6767-1.

Geisert, Arthur. 1986. *Pigs from A to Z.* Boston: Houghton Mifflin. ISBN 0-395-38509-1.

George, Jean Craighead. 1984. *One Day in the Alpine Tundra.* Illustrated by Walter Gaffney-Kessell. New York: Thomas Y. Crowell. ISBN 0-690-04325-2.

Geras, Adele. 1990. *My Grandmother's Stories: A Collection of Jewish Folk Tales.* Illustrated by Jael Jordan. New York: Alfred A. Knopf. ISBN 0-679-80910-4.

Gherman, Beverly. 1986. *Georgia O'Keeffe: The Wideness and Wonder of Her World.* New York: Atheneum. ISBN 0-689-31164-8.

————. 1992. *E. B. White: Some Writer!* New York: Atheneum. ISBN 0-689-31672-0.

Gibbons, Gail. 1984. *Fire! Fire!* New York: Thomas Y. Crowell. ISBN 0-690-04417-8.

Goble, Paul. 1988. *Her Seven Brothers.* New York: Bradbury Press. ISBN 0-02-737960-4.

————. 1990. *Iktomi and the Buffalo Skull: A Plains Indian Story.* New York: Orchard Books. ISBN 0-531-05911-1.

Goffstein, M. B. 1986. *Our Snowman.* New York: Harper and Row. ISBN 0-06-022152-6.

————. 1986. *School of Names.* New York: Harper and Row. ISBN 0-06-021984-X.

Goodall, John S. 1983. *Above and Below Stairs.* New York: Atheneum. ISBN 0-689-50238-9.

Goor, Ron, and Nancy Goor. 1983. *Signs.* New York: Thomas Y. Crowell. ISBN 0-690-04354-6.

————. 1986. *Pompeii: Exploring a Roman Ghost Town.* New York: Thomas Y. Crowell. ISBN 0-690-04515-8.

Greenfield, Eloise. 1991. *Night on Neighborhood Street.* Illustrated by Jan Spivey Gilchrist. New York: Dial Books. ISBN 0-8037-0777-0.

Grifalconi, Ann. 1987. *Darkness and the Butterfly.* Boston: Little, Brown. ISBN 0-316-32863-4.

Guiberson, Brenda. 1991. *Cactus Hotel.* Illustrated by Megan Lloyd. New York: Henry Holt. ISBN 0-8050-1333-4.

Hamilton, Virginia. 1983. *The Magical Adventures of Pretty Pearl.* New York: Harper and Row. ISBN 0-06-022186-0.

————. 1985. *The People Could Fly: American Black Folktales.* Illustrated by Leo Dillon and Diane Dillon. New York: Alfred A. Knopf. ISBN 0-394-86925-7.

————. 1988. *Anthony Burns: The Defeat and Triumph of a Fugitive Slave.* New York: Alfred A. Knopf. ISBN 0-394-98185-5.

Harvey, Brett. 1986. *My Prairie Year: Based on the Diary of Elenore Plaisted.* Illustrated by Deborah Kogan Ray. New York: Holiday House. ISBN 0-8234-0604-0.

————. 1987. *Immigrant Girl: Becky of Eldridge Street.* Illustrated by Deborah Kogan Ray. New York: Holiday House. ISBN 0-8234-0638-5.

He Liyi, translator. 1986. *The Spring of Butterflies and Other Folktales of China's Minority Peoples.* Edited by Neil Philip. Illustrated by Pan Aiqing and Li Zhao. New York: Lothrop, Lee and Shepard. ISBN 0-688-06192-3.

Heide, Florence Parry, and Judith Heide Gilliland. 1990. *The Day of Ahmed's Secret.* Illustrated by Ted Lewin. New York: Lothrop, Lee and Shepard. ISBN 0-688-08894-5.

Henkes, Kevin. 1991. *Chrysanthemum.* New York: Greenwillow Books. ISBN 0-688-09700-6.

Hepworth, Catherine. 1992. *Antics! An Alphabet of Ants.* New York: G. P. Putnam's Sons. ISBN 0-399-21862-9.

Highwater, Jamake. 1984. *Legend Days.* New York: Harper and Row. ISBN 0-06-022303-0.

Hirst, Robin, and Sally Hirst. 1990. *My Place in Space.* Illustrated by Roland Harvey and Joe Levine. New York: Orchard Books. ISBN 0-531-05859-X.

Ho, Minfong. 1991. *The Clay Marble.* New York: Farrar, Straus and Giroux. ISBN 0-374-31340-7.

Hoffman, Mary. 1991. *Amazing Grace.* Illustrated by Caroline Binch. New York: Dial Books. ISBN 0-8037-1040-2.

Hogrogian, Nonny. 1988. *The Cat Who Loved to Sing.* New York: Alfred A. Knopf. ISBN 0-394-99004-8.

Hoguet, Susan Ramsay. 1983. *I Unpacked My Grandmother's Trunk: A Picture Book Game.* New York: E. P. Dutton. ISBN 0-525-44069-0.

———. 1986. *Solomon Grundy.* New York: E. P. Dutton. ISBN 0-525-44239-1.

Hooks, William H. 1987. *Moss Gown.* Illustrated by Donald Carrick. New York: Clarion Books. ISBN 0-89919-460-5.

———. 1990. *The Ballad of Belle Dorcas.* Illustrated by J. Brian Pinkney. New York: Alfred A. Knopf. ISBN 0-394-84645-1.

Hopkins, Lee Bennett. 1983. *A Song in Stone: City Poems.* Photographs by Anna Held Audette. New York: Thomas Y. Crowell. ISBN 0-690-04269-8.

Houston, Gloria. 1992. *My Great-Aunt Arizona.* Illustrated by Susan Condie Lamb. New York: HarperCollins. ISBN 0-06-022606-4.

Howe, James. 1983. *The Celery Stalks at Midnight.* Illustrated by Leslie Morrill. New York: Atheneum. ISBN 0-689-30987-2.

Hudson, Jan. 1989. *Sweetgrass.* New York: Philomel Books. ISBN 0-399-21721-5.

Hughes, Shirley. 1985. *Noisy.* New York: Lothrop, Lee and Shepard. ISBN 0-688-04203-1.

————. 1988. *Out and About.* New York: Lothrop, Lee and Shepard. ISBN 0-688-07691-2.

Hunt, Irene. 1985. *The Everlasting Hills.* New York: Charles Scribner's Sons. ISBN 0-684-18340-4.

Hutchins, Pat. 1986. *The Doorbell Rang.* New York: Greenwillow Books. ISBN 0-688-05251-7.

Ivimey, John W. 1987. *The Complete Story of the Three Blind Mice.* Illustrated by Paul Galdone. New York: Clarion Books. ISBN 0-89919-481-8.

Janeczko, Paul B. 1990. *The Place My Words Are Looking For: What Poets Say About and Through Their Work.* New York: Bradbury Press. ISBN 0-02-747671-5.

Johnston, Tony. 1987. *Whale Song: A Celebration of Counting.* Illustrated by Ed Young. New York: G. P. Putnam's Sons. ISBN 0-399-21402-X.

Kaye, Cathryn Berger. 1985. *Word Works: Why the Alphabet Is a Kid's Best Friend.* Illustrated by Martha Weston. Boston: Little, Brown. ISBN 0-316-48376-1.

Kennedy, X. J. 1985. *The Forgetful Wishing Well: Poems for Young People.* New York: Atheneum. ISBN 0-689-50317-2.

————. 1986. *Brats.* New York: Atheneum. ISBN 0-689-50392-X.

Kesey, Ken. 1990. *Little Tricker the Squirrel Meets Big Double the Bear.* Illustrated by Barry Moser. New York: Viking. ISBN 0-670-81136-X.

Khalsa, Dayal Kaur. 1986. *Tales of a Gambling Grandma.* New York: C. N. Potter. ISBN 0-51756-137-9.

Kimmel, Eric A. 1989. *Hershel and the Hanukkah Goblins.* Illustrated by Trina Schart Hyman. New York: Holiday House. ISBN 0-8234-0769-1.

Konigsburg, E. L. 1986. *Up from Jericho Tel.* New York: Atheneum. ISBN 0-689-31194-X.

Koontz, Robin Michal. 1988. *This Old Man: The Counting Song.* New York: Dodd, Mead. ISBN 0-396-09120-2.

Korty, Carol. 1986. *Writing Your Own Plays: Creating, Adapting, Improvising.* New York: Charles Scribner's Sons. ISBN 0-684-18470-2.

Kroll, Steven. 1988. *Happy Father's Day.* Illustrated by Marylin Hafner. New York: Holiday House. ISBN 0-8234-0671-7.

Lankford, Mary D. 1992. *Hopscotch around the World.* Illustrated by Karen Milone-Dugan. New York: William Morrow. ISBN 0-688-08419-2.

Lasky, Kathryn. 1983. *Sugaring Time.* Photographs by Christopher G. Knight. New York: Macmillan. ISBN 0-02-751680-6.

————. 1992. *Surtsey: The Newest Place on Earth.* Photographs by Christopher G. Knight. New York: Hyperion Books. ISBN 1-56282-300-0.

Lattimore, Deborah Nourse. 1987. *The Flame of Peace: A Tale of the Aztecs.* New York: Harper and Row. ISBN 0-06-023708-2.

Lauber, Patricia. 1985. *Tales Mummies Tell.* New York: Thomas Y. Crowell. ISBN 0-690-04388-0.

————. 1989. *The News about Dinosaurs.* New York: Bradbury Press. ISBN 0-02-754520-2.

Leaf, Margaret. 1987. *Eyes of the Dragon.* Illustrated by Ed Young. New York: Lothrop, Lee and Shepard. ISBN 0-688-06155-9.

Legum, Margaret Ronay. 1985. *Mailbox, Quailbox.* Illustrated by Robert Shetterly. New York: Atheneum. ISBN 0-689-31136-2.

Lewis, Claudia Louise. 1987. *Long Ago in Oregon.* Illustrated by Joel Fontaine. New York: Harper and Row. ISBN 0-06-023839-9.

Lewis, Richard. 1988. *In the Night, Still Dark.* Illustrated by Ed Young. New York: Atheneum. ISBN 0-689-31310-1.

Livingston, Myra Cohn. 1984. *Sky Songs.* Illustrated by Leonard Everett Fisher. New York: Holiday House. ISBN 0-8234-0502-8.

————. 1985. *A Learical Lexicon: From the Works of Edward Lear.* Illustrated by Joseph Low. New York: Atheneum. ISBN 0-689-50318-0.

————. 1986. *Earth Songs.* Illustrated by Leonard Everett Fisher. New York: Holiday House. ISBN 0-8234-0615-6.

————. 1988. *There Was a Place and Other Poems.* New York: Margaret K. McElderry Books. ISBN 0-689-50464-0.

Lobel, Anita. 1990. *Alison's Zinnia.* New York: Greenwillow Books. ISBN 0-688-08866-X.

Lobel, Arnold. 1983. *The Book of Pigericks.* New York: Harper and Row. ISBN 0-06-023982-4.

————. 1984. *The Rose in My Garden.* New York: Greenwillow Books. ISBN 0-688-02586-2.

————. 1985. *Whiskers and Rhymes.* New York: Greenwillow Books. ISBN 0-688-03835-2.

Lord, Bette Bao. 1984. *In the Year of the Boar and Jackie Robinson.* Illustrated by Marc Simont. New York: Harper and Row. ISBN 0-06-024003-2.

MacDonald, Suse. 1986. *Alphabatics.* New York: Bradbury Press. ISBN 0-02-761520-0.

MacLachlan, Patricia. 1985. *Sarah, Plain and Tall.* New York: Harper and Row. ISBN 0-06-024101-2.

————. 1991. *Journey.* New York: Delacorte Press. ISBN 0-385-30427-7.

Magnus, Erica. 1984. *Old Lars.* Minneapolis: Carolrhoda Books. ISBN 0-87614-253-6.

Mahy, Margaret. 1987. *17 Kings and 42 Elephants.* Illustrated by Patricia MacCarthy. New York: Dial Books. ISBN 0-8037-0458-5.

———. 1989. *The Blood-and-Thunder Adventure on Hurricane Peak.* Illustrated by Wendy Smith. New York: Margaret K. McElderry Books. ISBN 0-689-50488-8.

Martin, Bill, Jr. 1991. *Polar Bear, Polar Bear, What Do You Hear?* Illustrated by Eric Carle. New York: Henry Holt. ISBN 0-8050-1759-3.

Martin, Bill, Jr., and John Archambault. 1985. *The Ghost-Eye Tree.* Illustrated by Ted Rand. New York: Henry Holt. ISBN 0-8050-0208-1.

———. 1987. *Knots on a Counting Rope.* Illustrated by Ted Rand. New York: Henry Holt. ISBN 0-8050-0571-4.

———. 1988. *Listen to the Rain.* Illustrated by James R. Endicott. New York: Henry Holt. ISBN 0-8050-0682-6.

———. 1989. *Chicka Chicka Boom Boom.* Illustrated by Lois Ehlert. New York: Simon and Schuster. ISBN 0-671-67949-X.

Martin, Rafe. 1985. *Foolish Rabbit's Big Mistake.* Illustrated by Ed Young. New York: G. P. Putnam's Sons. ISBN 0-399-21178-0.

McCully, Emily Arnold. 1984. *Picnic.* New York: Harper and Row. ISBN 0-06-024099-7.

McDonald, Megan. 1990. *Is This a House for Hermit Crab?* Illustrated by S. D. Schindler. New York: Orchard Books. ISBN 0-531-05855-7.

McKay, Hilary. 1992. *The Exiles.* New York: Margaret K. McElderry Books. ISBN 0-689-50555-8.

McKissack, Patricia. 1986. *Flossie and the Fox.* Illustrated by Rachel Isadora. New York: Dial Books. ISBN 0-8037-0250-7.

———. 1991. *A Million Fish—More or Less.* Illustrated by Dena Schutzer. New York: Alfred A. Knopf. ISBN 0-679-80692-X.

McMillan, Bruce. 1992. *The Baby Zoo.* New York: Scholastic. ISBN 0-590-44634-7.

McPhail, David M. 1985. *The Dream Child.* New York: E. P. Dutton. ISBN 0-525-44366-5.

———. 1985. *Farm Morning.* San Diego: Harcourt Brace Jovanovich. ISBN 0-15-227299-2.

Meddaugh, Susan. 1992. *Martha Speaks.* Boston: Houghton Mifflin. ISBN 0-395-63313-3.

Meltzer, Milton. 1985. *Dorothea Lange: Life through the Camera.* Illustrated by Donna Diamond and Dorothea Lange. New York: Viking. ISBN 0-670-28047-X.

Merriam, Eve. 1986. *Fresh Paint: New Poems.* Illustrated by David Frampton. New York: Macmillan. ISBN 0-02-766860-6.

———. 1987. *Halloween ABC.* Illustrated by Lane Smith. New York: Macmillan. ISBN 0-02-766870-3.

————. 1992. *Fighting Words.* Illustrated by David Small. New York: William Morrow. ISBN 0-688-09677-8.

Mollel, Tololwa M. 1990. *The Orphan Boy: A Maasai Story.* Illustrated by Paul Morin. New York: Clarion Books. ISBN 0-89919-985-2.

Moore, Inga. 1991. *Six-Dinner Sid.* New York: Simon and Schuster. ISBN 0-671-73199-8.

Moore, Lilian. 1988. *I'll Meet You at the Cucumbers.* Illustrated by Sharon Wooding. New York: Atheneum. ISBN 0-689-31243-1.

Morrison, Lillian. 1985. *The Break Dance Kids: Poems of Sport, Motion, and Locomotion.* New York: Lothrop, Lee and Shepard. ISBN 0-688-04553-7.

Moscovitch, Rosalie. 1985. *What's in a Word? A Dictionary of Daffy Definitions.* Boston: Houghton Mifflin. ISBN 0-395-38922-4.

Munro, Roxie. 1985. *The Inside-Outside Book of New York City.* New York: Dodd, Mead. ISBN 0-396-08513-X.

Nelson, Drew. 1991. *Wild Voices.* Illustrated by John Schoenherr. New York: Philomel Books. ISBN 0-399-21798-3.

Nelson, Vaunda Micheaux. 1988. *Always Gramma.* Illustrated by Kimanne Uhler. New York: G. P. Putnam's Sons. ISBN 0-399-21542-5.

Neumeier, Marty, and Byron Glaser. 1985. *Action Alphabet.* New York: Greenwillow Books. ISBN 0-688-05703-9.

Nixon, Joan Lowery. 1988. *If You Were a Writer.* Illustrated by Bruce Degen. New York: Four Winds Press. ISBN 0-02-768210-2.

O'Keefe, Susan Heyboer. 1989. *One Hungry Monster: A Counting Book in Rhyme.* Illustrated by Lynn Munsinger. Boston: Joy Street Books. ISBN 0-316-63385-2.

O'Neill, Catharine. 1989. *Mrs. Dunphy's Dog.* New York: Puffin Books. ISBN 0-14-050622-5.

Ormerod, Jan. 1985. *Reading.* New York: Lothrop, Lee and Shepard. ISBN 0-688-04127-2.

Orr, Katherine Shelley. 1990. *My Grandpa and the Sea.* Minneapolis: Carolrhoda Books. ISBN 0-87614-409-1.

Parnall, Peter. 1989. *Quiet.* New York: William Morrow. ISBN 0-688-08204-1.

Paterson, Katherine. 1991. *Lyddie.* New York: E. P. Dutton. ISBN 0-525-67338-5.

Paulsen, Gary. 1983. *Dancing Carl.* Scarsdale, NY: Bradbury Press. ISBN 0-02-770210-3.

————. 1987. *Hatchet.* New York: Bradbury Press. ISBN 0-02-770130-1.

————. 1988. *The Island.* New York: Orchard Books. ISBN 0-531-05749-6.

————. 1989. *The Winter Room.* New York: Orchard Books. ISBN 0-531-05839-5.

————. 1990. *Woodsong.* Illustrated by Ruth Wright Paulsen. New York: Bradbury Press. ISBN 0-02-770221-9.

Polacco, Patricia. 1990. *Thunder Cake.* New York: Philomel Books. ISBN 0-399-22231-6.

Purviance, Susan, and Marcia O'Shell. 1988. *Alphabet Annie Announces an All-American Album.* Illustrated by Ruth Brunner-Strosser. Boston: Houghton Mifflin. ISBN 0-395-48070-1.

Rankin, Laura. 1991. *The Handmade Alphabet.* New York: Dial Books. ISBN 0-8037-0974-9.

Reeder, Carolyn. 1989. *Shades of Gray.* New York: Macmillan. ISBN 0-02-775810-9.

Ringgold, Faith. 1991. *Tar Beach.* New York: Crown Publishers. ISBN 0-517-58030-6.

Robertson, Joanne. 1991. *Sea Witches.* New York: Dial Books. ISBN 0-8037-1070-4.

Roop, Peter, and Connie Roop. 1985. *Keep the Lights Burning, Abbie.* Illustrated by Peter E. Hanson. Minneapolis: Carolrhoda Books. ISBN 0-87614-275-7.

Root, Phyllis. 1992. *The Listening Silence.* Illustrated by Dennis McDermott. New York: HarperCollins. ISBN 0-06-025092-5.

Rosen, Michael. 1989. *We're Going on a Bear Hunt.* Illustrated by Helen Oxenbury. New York: Margaret K. McElderry Books. ISBN 0-689-50476-4.

Roth, Susan L., and Ruth Phang. 1984. *Patchwork Tales.* New York: Atheneum. ISBN 0-689-31053-6.

Ryder, Joanne. 1985. *Inside Turtle's Shell and Other Poems of the Field.* Illustrated by Susan Bonners. New York: Macmillan. ISBN 0-02-778010-4.

————. 1992. *Dancers in the Garden.* Illustrated by Judith Lopez. San Francisco: Sierra Club Books. ISBN 0-87156-578-1.

Rylant, Cynthia. 1984. *This Year's Garden.* Illustrated by Mary Szilagyi. Scarsdale, NY: Bradbury Press. ISBN 0-02-777970-X.

————. 1984. *Waiting to Waltz: A Childhood.* Illustrated by Stephen Gammell. Scarsdale, NY: Bradbury Press. ISBN 0-02-778000-7.

————. 1985. *Every Living Thing: Stories.* Illustrated by S. D. Schindler. New York: Bradbury Press. ISBN 0-02-777200-4.

————. 1986. *A Fine White Dust.* New York: Bradbury Press. ISBN 0-02-777240-3.

————. 1986. *Night in the Country.* Illustrated by Mary Szilagyi. New York: Bradbury Press. ISBN 0-02-777210-1.

————. 1987. *Children of Christmas: Stories for the Season.* Illustrated by S. D. Schindler. New York: Orchard Books. ISBN 0-531-05706-2.

————. 1991. *Appalachia: The Voices of Sleeping Birds.* Illustrated by Barry Moser. San Diego: Harcourt Brace Jovanovich. ISBN 0-15-201605-8.

————. 1992. *Missing May.* New York: Orchard Books. ISBN 0-531-05996-0.

Salisbury, Graham. 1992. *Blue Skin of the Sea.* New York: Delacorte Press. ISBN 0-385-30596-6.

Sanders, Scott R. 1985. *Hear the Wind Blow: American Folk Songs Retold.* Illustrated by Ponder Goembel. New York: Bradbury Press. ISBN 0-02-778140-2.

San Souci, Robert D. 1989. *The Talking Eggs: A Folktale from the American South.* Illustrated by Jerry Pinkney. New York: Dial Books. ISBN 0-8037-0619-7.

Schwartz, Alvin. 1983. *Unriddling: All Sorts of Riddles to Puzzle Your Guessery.* Illustrated by Sue Truesdell. New York: Harper and Row. ISBN 0-06-446057-6.

————. 1992. *And the Green Grass Grew All Around: Folk Poetry from Everyone.* Illustrated by Sue Truesdell. New York: HarperCollins. ISBN 0-06-022757-5.

Selden, Bernice. 1983. *The Mill Girls: Lucy Larcom, Harriet Hanson Robinson, Sarah G. Bagley.* New York: Atheneum. ISBN 0-689-31005-6.

Sender, Ruth Minsky. 1988. *To Life.* New York: Macmillan. ISBN 0-02-781831-4.

Shannon, George. 1985. *Stories to Solve: Folktales from Around the World.* Illustrated by Peter Sis. New York: Greenwillow Books. ISBN 0-688-04303-8.

Siebert, Diane. 1989. *Heartland.* Paintings by Wendell Minor. New York: Thomas Y. Crowell. ISBN 0-690-04730-4.

Singer, Marilyn. 1989. *Turtle in July.* Illustrated by Jerry Pinkney. New York: Macmillan. ISBN 0-02-782881-6.

Slepian, Jan. 1988. *The Broccoli Tapes.* New York: Philomel Books. ISBN 0-399-21712-6.

Smith, Doris Buchanan. 1986. *Return to Bitter Creek.* New York: Viking. ISBN 0-670-80783-4.

————. 1989. *Voyages.* New York: Viking. ISBN 0-670-80739-7.

Snyder, Zilpha Keatley. 1985. *The Changing Maze.* Illustrated by Charles Mikolaycak. New York: Macmillan. ISBN 0-02-785900-2.

————. 1990. *Libby on Wednesdays.* New York: Delacorte Press. ISBN 0-385-29979-6.

Sperling, Susan Kelz. 1985. *Murfles and Wink-a-Peeps: Funny, Old Words for Kids.* Illustrated by Tom Bloom. New York: C. N. Potter. ISBN 0-517-55659-6.

Spier, Peter. 1986. *Dreams.* New York: Doubleday. ISBN 0-385-19336-X.

Spinelli, Jerry. 1990. *Maniac Magee: A Novel.* Boston: Little, Brown. ISBN 0-316-80722-2.

Springer, Nancy. 1992. *The Friendship Song.* New York: Atheneum. ISBN 0-689-31727-1.

Staines, Bill. 1989. *All God's Critters Got a Place in the Choir.* Illustrated by Margot Zemach. New York: E. P. Dutton. ISBN 0-525-44469-6.

Stanley, Diane. 1983. *The Conversation Club.* New York: Macmillan. ISBN 0-02-786740-4.

Stanley, Diane, and Peter Vennema. 1992. *Bard of Avon: The Story of William Shakespeare.* Illustrated by Diane Stanley. New York: William Morrow. ISBN 0-688-09108-3.

Steig, Jeanne. 1992. *Alpha Beta Chowder.* Illustrated by Willliam Steig. New York: HarperCollins. ISBN 0-06-205006-0.

Steig, William. 1986. *Brave Irene.* New York: Farrar, Straus and Giroux. ISBN 0-374-30947-7.

Stevens, Janet. 1987. *The Town Mouse and the Country Mouse: An Aesop Fable.* New York: Holiday House. ISBN 0-8234-0633-4.

Stevenson, James. 1984. *Yuck!* New York: Greenwillow Books. ISBN 0-688-03829-8.

Summerfield, Geoffrey. 1983. *Welcome and Other Poems.* Illustrated by Karen Usborne. London: A. Deutsch. ISBN 0-233-97528-4.

Tchudi, Susan J., and Stephen Tchudi. 1984. *The Young Writer's Handbook.* New York: Charles Scribner's Sons. ISBN 0-684-18090-1.

Temple, Frances. 1992. *Taste of Salt: A Story of Modern Haiti.* New York: Orchard Books. ISBN 0-531-05459-4.

Terban, Marvin. 1985. *Too Hot to Hoot: Funny Palindrome Riddles.* Illustrated by Giulio Maestro. New York: Clarion Books. ISBN 0-89919-319-6.

Testa, Fulvio. 1983. *If You Look Around You.* New York: Dial Books. ISBN 0-8037-0003-2.

Tompert, Ann. 1990. *Grandfather Tang's Story.* Illustrated by Robert Andrew Parker. New York: Crown Publishers. ISBN 0-517-57487-X.

Turner, Ann. 1985. *Dakota Dugout.* Illustrated by Ronald Himler. New York: Macmillan. ISBN 0-02-789700-1.

———. 1986. *Street Talk.* Illustrated by Catherine Stock. Boston: Houghton Mifflin. ISBN 0-395-39971-8.

———. 1987. *Nettie's Trip South.* Illustrated by Ronald Himler. New York: Macmillan. ISBN 0-02-789240-9.

————. 1991. *Rosemary's Witch.* New York: HarperCollins. ISBN 0-06-026127-7.

Van Allsburg, Chris. 1984. *The Mysteries of Harris Burdick.* Boston: Houghton Mifflin. ISBN 0-395-35393-9.

————. 1986. *The Stranger.* Boston: Houghton Mifflin. ISBN 0-395-42331-7.

————. 1987. *The Z Was Zapped: A Play in Twenty-Six Acts.* Boston: Houghton Mifflin. ISBN 0-395-44612-0.

Vande Velde, Vivian. 1985. *A Hidden Magic.* Illustrated by Trina Schart Hyman. New York: Crown Publishers. ISBN 0-517-55534-4.

Van Laan, Nancy. 1987. *The Big Fat Worm.* Illustrated by Marisabina Russo. New York: Alfred A. Knopf. ISBN 0-394-98763-2.

————. 1990. *Possum Come A-Knockin'.* Illustrated by George Booth. New York: Alfred A. Knopf. ISBN 0-394-82206-4.

Ventura, Piero. 1984. *Great Painters.* New York: G. P. Putnam's Sons. ISBN 0-399-21115-2.

Waddell, Martin. 1992. *Farmer Duck.* Illustrated by Helen Oxenbury. Cambridge, MA: Candlewick Press. ISBN 1-56402-009-6.

Wallace, Ian. 1988. *Morgan the Magnificent.* New York: Macmillan. ISBN 0-689-50441-1.

Wallace-Brodeur, Ruth. 1989. *Stories from the Big Chair.* Illustrated by Diane DeGroat. New York: Margaret K. McElderry Books. ISBN 0-689-50481-0.

Wiesner, David. 1991. *Tuesday.* New York: Clarion Books. ISBN 0-395-55113-7.

Willard, Nancy. 1990. *The High Rise Glorious Skittle Skat Roarious Sky Pie Angel Food Cake.* Illustrated by Richard Jesse Watson. San Diego: Harcourt Brace Jovanovich. ISBN 0-15-234332-6.

————. 1991. *Pish, Posh, Said Hieronymous Bosch.* Illustrated by Leo Dillon and Diane Dillon. San Diego: Harcourt Brace Jovanovich. ISBN 0-15-262210-1.

Williams, Karen Lynn. 1990. *Galimoto.* Illustrated by Catherine Stock. New York: Lothrop, Lee and Shepard. ISBN 0-688-08789-2.

Williams, Linda. 1986. *The Little Old Lady Who Was Not Afraid of Anything.* Illustrated by Megan Lloyd. New York: Thomas Y. Crowell. ISBN 0-690-04584-0.

Williams, Terry Tempest. 1985. *Between Cattails.* Illustrated by Peter Parnall. New York: Charles Scribner's Sons. ISBN 0-684-18309-9.

Williams, Terry Tempest, and Ted Major. 1984. *The Secret Language of Snow.* Illustrated by Jennifer Dewey. San Francisco: Sierra Club/ Pantheon Books. ISBN 0-394-86574-X.

Williams, Vera B., and Jennifer Williams. 1987. *Stringbean's Trip to the Shining Sea.* New York: Greenwillow Books. ISBN 0-688-07162-7.

Williamson, Duncan. 1983. *Fireside Tales of the Traveller Children: Twelve Scottish Stories.* Illustrated by Alan B. Herriot. New York: Harmony Books. ISBN 0-517-55852-1.

Wilson, Budge. 1992. *The Leaving and Other Stories.* New York: Philomel Books. ISBN 0-399-21878-5.

Winter, Jeanette. 1988. *Follow the Drinking Gourd.* New York: Alfred A. Knopf. ISBN 0-394-99694-1.

Wolff, Ashley. 1985. *Only the Cat Saw.* New York: Dodd, Mead. ISBN 0-396-08727-2.

Wood, Audrey. 1987. *Heckedy Peg.* Illustrated by Don Wood. San Diego: Harcourt Brace Jovanovich. ISBN 0-15-233678-8.

————. 1988. *Elbert's Bad Word.* Illustrated by Audrey Wood and Don Wood. San Diego: Harcourt Brace Jovanovich. ISBN 0-15-225320-3.

Worth, Valerie. 1986. *Small Poems Again.* Illustrated by Natalie Babbitt. New York: Farrar, Straus and Giroux. ISBN 0-374-37074-5.

Wrightson, Patricia. 1985. *Night Outside.* Illustrated by Beth Peck. New York: Atheneum. ISBN 0-689-50363-6.

Yolen, Jane. 1984. *Children of the Wolf: A Novel.* New York: Viking. ISBN 0-670-21763-8.

————. 1986. *Ring of Earth: A Child's Book of Seasons.* Illustrated by John C. Wallner. San Diego: Harcourt Brace Jovanovich. ISBN 0-15-267140-4.

————. 1987. *Piggins.* Illustrated by Jane Dyer. San Diego: Harcourt Brace Jovanovich. ISBN 0-15-261685-3.

————. 1988. *Best Witches: Poems for Halloween.* Illustrated by Elise Primavera. New York: G. P. Putnam's Sons. ISBN 0-399-21539-5.

————. 1989. *Dove Isabeau.* Illustrated by Dennis Nolan. San Diego: Harcourt Brace Jovanovich. ISBN 0-15-224131-0.

————. 1990. *Bird Watch: A Book of Poetry.* Illustrated by Ted Lewin. New York: Philomel Books. ISBN 0-399-21612-X.

Ziefert, Harriet. 1986. *Sarah's Questions.* Illustrated by Susan Bonners. New York: Lothrop, Lee and Shepard. ISBN 0-688-05614-8.

Editors

Amy A. McClure is associate professor of education at Ohio Wesleyan University, where she teaches courses in reading, language arts, and children's literature and directs the university honors program. She is a former chair of the Notable Children's Trade Books in the Language Arts Committee. She is also the author of *Sunrises and Songs: Reading and Writing Poetry in an Elementary Classroom* and book chapters and articles on children's response to literature, using poetry with children, whole language teaching strategies, and other related topics. Dr. McClure was named NCTE's Promising Young Researcher in 1985.

Janice V. Kristo is associate professor of education at the University of Maine, where she teaches courses in reading, language arts, and children's literature. She is a former chair of the Notable Children's Trade Books in the Language Arts Committee. She has written articles on children's response to literature, evaluation of whole language teachers, integration of the language arts, and classroom-based research.

Contributors

Carol Avery is a classroom teacher in Lancaster, Pennsylvania. She is also a literacy consultant to schools and a speaker on whole language, reading and writing processes, and children's literature. She has taught high school English and has been a children's librarian. In addition to journal articles, book chapters, and journal columns, she has written . . . *And with a Light Touch: Learning about Reading, Writing, and Teaching from First Graders.*

Carolyn J. Bauer is professor of curriculum at Oklahoma State University and director of the NEH/OSU Interdisciplinary Teaching Project. She has taught in elementary school classrooms, served as a library media specialist, worked as a K–8 children's literature consultant, and presented frequently at professional conferences. In addition, she has served on the Newbery Committee, the Caldecott Committee, NCTE's Notable Books in the Language Arts Committee, and Oklahoma's Sequoyah Children's Book Award Committee.

Joan I. Glazer is professor of education at Rhode Island College, where she teaches courses in children's literature and language arts methods. She has taught at the elementary level and has served as a consultant on literature and language in New England elementary and middle schools. She is the author of *Literature for Young Children* and *Introduction to Children's Literature* as well as articles in *Language Arts, The Reading Teacher,* and other professional journals.

Cheryl Grossman is associate professor of teacher education at the University of Missouri–Kansas City. She has taught elementary school and was an integrated arts specialist for the New York City public schools. Dr. Grossman is co-author of *Jewish Literature for Children: A Teaching Guide* and has additional publications in arts education and bibliotherapy. She also served on the editorial board of *Clinical Pediatrics.* She is currently developing a teacher training program in the arts in collaboration with performing and visual artists in the Kansas City area.

Darwin L. Henderson is associate professor of literacy and language in the school of education at Purdue University. He has taught preschool and elementary children and is a former elementary school counselor. His articles, interviews, and book reviews have appeared in *Language Arts, The Reading Teacher, Children's Literature in Education, Children's Literature Association Quarterly,* and *The ALAN Review.* He is the co-editor of a forthcoming book on African, Caribbean, and African American poetry for the middle grades. He is currently a member of the Children's Literature Assembly's advisory board.

Rachael Hungerford is assistant professor of education at Lycoming College in Williamsport, Pennsylvania. She has taught elementary school, worked as a children's librarian, and now teaches courses in reading, language arts, children's literature, and qualitative research. She is director of the Children's Literature Jubilee, a conference held annually at Lycoming College. She is also a member of the editorial review board of *The Reading Teacher*, has served as a member of the Notable Books in the Language Arts Committee for NCTE, and reviews for Stenhouse Publishers. Dr. Hungerford has published several articles and has co-edited the book *Journeying: Children Responding to Literature*. She is currently doing research in the areas of gender identity in preschool children and working class women and literacy.

Melissa Keenan is a doctoral student in literacy at the University of Maine. In addition to her studies, she teaches undergraduate and masters-level courses in literacy and consults with administrators and teachers in local schools. She taught sixth grade for two years in a rural public school in Pine Plains, New York, and third grade for five years in a Quaker school in Wilmington, Delaware. She received a B.A. in anthropology from Vassar and an M.A. in reading, writing, and literacy from the University of Pennsylvania.

Inga Kromann-Kelly is professor of elementary and secondary education at Washington State University. She has taught grades K–8 in the public schools. She is also past president of the Children's Literature Assembly of NCTE, past United States editor of the IBBY journal *Bookbird*, and has been consulting editor of *Child Study Journal*. Her professional activities include presentations at regional and national conferences of NCTE, IRA, and AERA; consultantships; articles; trade book and textbook reviews; and contributions to resource books devoted to literature for children and young people.

Linda Leonard Lamme is professor of education at the University of Florida, where she teaches courses in language arts and children's literature. She has taught elementary school and was a lecturer at Syracuse University before joining the faculty at the University of Florida. She holds bachelor's and master's degrees from the University of Illinois and a Ph.D. from Syracuse. Her publications include journal articles and several books, including *Raising Readers* and *Learning to Love Literature*. Her most recent book is *Literature-Based Moral Education*.

Susan Lehr is associate professor of education at Skidmore College, where she is chair of the department of education. She is an incoming president of the Children's Literature Assembly and author of the book *The Child's Developing Sense of Theme.*

Anthony L. Manna is associate professor in the department of teaching, leadership, and curriculum studies at Kent State University. He teaches children's literature, young adult literature, and English education.

Jill P. May is professor of literacy and languages in the school of education at Purdue University, where she teaches courses in children's literature. She has been an active member of the Children's Literature Association, the Modern Language Association, and the National Council of Teachers of English, serving on committees and executive boards of these groups. Previously she published *Films and Filmstrips for Language Arts: An Annotated Bibliography* and *Lloyd Alexander.* In addition, she had edited *Children and Their Literature: A Readings Book* and co-edited *Festschrift: A Ten Year Retrospective.* Professor May has published over fifty articles in national professional journals of English, library science, and folklore. She has served on editorial boards of journals for the Children's Literature Assembly, the Children's Literature Association, the National Association for the Preservation and Perpetuation of Storytelling, the Indiana Library Association, and Bookbird, Inc. As the Purdue Snodgrass Fellow, she received a two-year, half-time leave to develop a theory for model literary criticism programs for grades K–6. Currently she is working with area elementary school teachers to create literary studies programs in their schools.

Marilou R. Sorensen is associate professor of educational studies in the graduate school of education at the University of Utah. She teaches undergraduate and graduate classes in children's and young adult literature, early literacy, and reading and conducts seminars for schools, libraries, and community organizations. She has served in various positions in NCTE, IRA, and on the Caldecott Committee in ALA, presented in workshops for all three organizations, and written articles for their journals. Her special interest is the home-school-literature connection. She writes a weekly column for *The Desert News,* a Salt Lake newspaper, and publishes four full-page features annually about special issues in reading and literature for young readers.

Jon C. Stott is professor of English at the University of Alberta. He is author of *Mary Norton* (a biocritical study) and *Children's Literature from A to Z: A Guide for Teachers and Parents* and co-author of *Canadian Books for Children: A Guide to Authors and Illustrators* and *The Family of Stories: An Anthology of Children's Literature.* His articles on the study and teaching of children's literature have appeared in British, American, and Canadian journals. A member of the founding board and the first president of the Children's Literature Association, he has lectured in over one hundred Canadian and American cities and works regularly as a demonstrator/consultant in elementary and junior high classrooms and libraries.

Carl Tomlison is associate professor of education in the department of curriculum and instruction at Northern Illinois University, where he teaches courses in language arts and children's literature and is director of the language arts laboratory. He is co-author of the textbook *Essentials of Children's Literature,* author of the forthcoming *Children's Books from Other Countries,* and associate editor of the international journal of children's literature *Bookbird: World of Children's Books.* His research interests are literature across the curriculum and international children's literature.

Richard Van Dongen is director and associate dean of the division of innovative programs and professor of elementary education at the University of New Mexico. He has taught elementary school and is the faculty director for the Teacher Enhancement Program, a teacher development program for mid-career teachers. He has published articles in children's literature and was president of the Children's Literature Assembly of NCTE. He continues to be active in NCTE and on the United States Board of Books for Young People.

Sylvia Mergeler Vardell is currently associate professor at the University of Texas at Arlington, where she teaches courses in literature-based teaching of reading, multicultural children's literature, and teaching the writing process. In addition to book chapters and articles in *Language Arts, English Journal, The Reading Teacher, The New Advocate, Young Children,* and *Horn Book,* she has co-authored a chapter on reading aloud and responding to nonfiction in *Using Nonfiction Trade Books in the Elementary Classroom.* She also served on the NCTE committee that established the Orbis Pictus award for outstanding nonfiction for children. She has made numerous presentations at state, regional, national, and international conferences and has received grants from NCTE and the National Endowment for the Humanities. She taught at the University of Zimbabwe in Africa as a Fulbright scholar in 1989. She is currently editor of *The State of Reading,* journal of the Texas State Reading Association.